Intention

Intention

Lee Thayer

Library of Congress Control Number:		2019901004
ISBN:	Hardcover	978-1-7960-1260-6
	Softcover	978-1-7960-1259-0
	eBook	978-1-7960-1258-3

Print information available on the last page.

Rev. date: 02/08/2019

To order additional copies of this book, contact:
Xlibris
1-888-795-4274
www.Xlibris.com
Orders@Xlibris.com
787980

The road to hell is paved with [unfulfilled] intentions

CONTENTS

CONTENTS

1 Intention: An Orientation (of sorts)

It was my intention in this book to provoke my good readers into thinking more widely and deeply about the central concept of intention in all of our everyday affairs. If it is your intention to be thus provoked, then we will accomplish something mightily valuable together. All books are co-authored by their readers. It is the reader's *interpretation* of what the author meant that the reader walks away with. As the reader, whatever "sticks" to you in your reading can change your life. To come to terms with the idea of intention will certainly change the quality of your life. If that is what you, the reader, *intend* by thinking about what follows in this book you are holding in your hands, then we are on the "same page." If we aren't, may I ask you to think through your interpretation of what I have written in this book with our mutual intentions in mind?

One's intentions – *and what one does about them* – has these pivotal consequences:

- First, they permanently affect the quality of life of the person who has them, and does or does not act upon them.
- Second, they can significantly affect the relationships that person has with the people, things, and events of his or her world. Our intentions toward that world create how we see it and ourselves in it. One's intentions with respect to every other person one comes into communicative contact with influences them both.

- Third, (and therefore in the aggregate) our intentions and what we do about them will affect in some small or large way the destiny of the society we all share.

Although those consequences may occur simultaneously, it may be useful to consider them separately, beginning in the next chapter. Here, there is more useful orientation to be probed.

+++++

We can think of an intention as being somewhat like a New Year's Resolution. Or, we can think of intention as being an unspoken promise to oneself. Or, we can think of intention as being a sort of promise that we make to another, or to others. Our intentions are what we make our futures out of. Either that, or whatever happens to us in a given day will determine what (and who) we become in the future. The latter is a future-less life since the person is not the agent forging it. The world around him or her is by default the maker of their future – their lives.

The columnist Evan Esar quipped:

> *"Good intentions, like good eggs, soon spoil unless they are hatched."*

This seems like as good a place as any to start. Esar tells us (and this is really ancient wisdom) that there are two things to consider carefully: one is whether your intentions are "good" or not. The second is that a person's intentions – good *or* bad – spoil unless they are carried out. And the person is left sitting on spoiled eggs. And this will end up spoiling the person, as we will see.

So, what is a good intention, and how is it to be distinguished from a bad intention or from a lack of intention? A bad intention is one that is bad for the person who harbors it, and is bad (in its consequences) for the person, the persons, or the world which is the target of that intention. (Think Hitler, perhaps.) In other words, a good intention is one that is good for all of those who are affected by it. A bad intention is one that is bad for all of those who are affected by it, and it is bad for the destiny of the society in which it is exercised.

We all know the proverbial saying: The road to hell is paved with good intentions. "Good" here means that a person intended to do good, but somehow never got around to any doing with respect to his or her intention. All they therefore had left was a good intention and that was stillborn. So the implication is, as Esar intimated, that hell is your destiny if you don't follow through on good intentions. The metaphor is apt.

At a more practical level, we could gain a perspective on our subject from that perspective-monger Oscar Wilde. (Wilde stated that his work of art and his primary contribution to society was himself and his sayings.) A pertinent quip of his for equipping ourselves with a needed perspective is as follows:

> *"The worst work is always done with the best intentions."*

You could interpret this in several ways, but try this one: People don't have the intention of acquitting themselves with poor or meaningless work. On the other hand, people often have good intentions. But their intentions outpace their competence to do what has to be done.

They can thus have the best intentions, but end up doing shabby work. This seems to hold true in every domain of human endeavor. For example, a young person may say to herself, I think I'll be a concert pianist with the Chicago Symphony. There's certainly nothing wrong with that intention. But the distance between an intention and fulfilling it may be one of the longest distances people ever face. If you want to be selected onto the Winter Olympics team, you may have to undergo some training other than occasionally skiing. If you want to be a concert pianist, you may have to put in the 10,000 hours of practice that may be required to arrive there. If your intention is to be a world-class lover, spouse, and father, you may have to devote some years of designated practice in order to get there.

Obviously, most people have more concern with their comfort and status quo than they do for any kind of aspiration. Those are not the measure of any kind of human possibility. It is perhaps a good thing to have aspirations of some sort. But if you don't do what you have to do to bring those aspirations to fruition, they rot and sour in the hearts and minds of those who had them. The fact that most people express mild-to-severe dissatisfaction with their lives at mid-point is an expression of this rot. Their dissatisfactions, as mild as they may be, come from this rotting compost pile (of once-expressed intentions), not from the world they live in. The world they live in may afford them conditions that once were reserved for the gods – or for royalty. And if those conditions do not suit them, there is no one but them capable of changing those conditions (as George Bernard Shaw and William James have argued). Those people are awaiting a savior in Congress (or perhaps a pill) to change those conditions into conditions they will inevitably find fault with as before.

Jean Toomer, of mixed race and an acolyte of Gurdjieff, made this pithy observation:

"We are tired of not being intense."

It is intensity that illumines and energizes our lives. And intensity comes from actually trying all the time to fulfill one's intentions. Somnolence is a basic form of laziness – of a deeply ingrained indifference to life itself. Its cause is not a matter of not having intentions, but of not doing something positive about one's good intentions. Intending is not the same as doing something positive about one's diet – about making it a habit rather than a mere intention. We all have good intentions. A few people do what has to be done to carry out those good intentions. It requires both. An intention not incorrigibly carried out is what rots the soul. You've met people who seem not to have a soul – an inner being seeking to realize itself in the world outside their own heads. That's not because they don't have good intentions. It is that they are not persistently trying to fulfill them. The Catholic Church dubs the latter as "saints." But Buddhism asks that every person needs to aspire to be a saint – to *become* Buddha.

+++++

Good intentions do not realize themselves. If you are a parent or a boss or a teacher or a doctor or a minister, you have a moral obligation to make of people better humans today than they were yesterday, beginning with yourself. If your intention is to do good in your role, then you are obligated to do it. Like Moses, you are not handed the instructions about *how* to do good. You have to figure that out, given the circumstances and given your competencies. Just because you don't have a recipe for how to do it is no excuse for not doing it. That's what you have a mind for. If you haven't equipped your mind to deal with such an obligation, that would be a prerequisite condition.

Some people might be tempted to substitute a word like "wish" or "desire" for intention. Yet *intention* has no substitute, no synonym. Intention carries with it the implication of some action. There is a sense of commitment in intention that does not exist for the passive notions of wishing or desiring or even aspiring. Those are internal states of a person. An intention is like a destination. One knows what has to be done. It's just a matter of doing it. Wishes die like stars do. If your intention is to get from point A to point B, the test is whether or not you got to point B. If you never visualize the path – or take the path visualized – your intention is just for talking purposes, talking to oneself or to others. People talk far more about their intentions than they do about their achievements. We don't think of a wish as demanding anything but some magic. Intention is not a magical term in the same sense. It is more like a promise that one makes to oneself, or to others.

+++++

A person's intentions are likely to be tinged with his or her ideological biases. And, since these are endorsed by the popular culture, they change over time, moving perhaps from left to right, or from right to left.

For example, as our civilization has evolved into increasing permissiveness and self-centeredness, we are more likely to find endorsement of our own biases in the more liberal rather than philosophies like stoicism that carried heavy personal responsibility. So Rousseau is more likely to be taught in school than is, say, Seneca. So a reader finds there more justification for his or her intentions (they have to be legitimated by *some* source, and in a radical democracy like our own, that source is likely to be whatever is popular). Rousseau was an early proponent of democracy and of the permissiveness that went with it. So it is understandable that he wrote, in his *Confessions*:

> *"I may not always have done what was right,*
> *but at least I had good intentions."*

This is probably more of a reflection of the changing times rather than of any philosophy extant at the time. But what he is pointing to is the subtle way in which *intentions began to be more important than the consequences in the popular culture*. Today, if you have good intentions, you might be forgiven the consequences. It probably is not intentional when someone overdoses on drugs and dies as a result. As the predatory legal outlook would have it: If that is not what the person intended, then it must have been due to circumstances beyond his or her control, and therefore not something for which they should be considered culpable. There was a time when, if someone did something wrong, they could argue that "The Devil made me do it." That was transitional. It was one's private "devil" and he or she should have better trained personal devils. So they had *some* responsibility. In our day, attributing some misdeed to addiction, for example, takes away any personal responsibility for the consequences. Years ago it was the consequences that mattered. Today it is intention. If a child did not intend to break the plate, then the child should be forgiven. It may be but a subtle shift in perspective, but it has radically altered the way we live and how difficult has become our attempts to deal with right and wrong.

People today have little or no responsibility for how their own lives turn out (since they are free – economically and legally – to abdicate that responsibility), *or* for the destiny of our civilization itself. When you no longer have to be concerned about how your actions affect the destiny of the society, it is likely that our society (the "Mother" on whom we all depend) will cease to be concerned in any vital way about your own personal and/or collective destiny. And isn't this exactly what is happening? When the self eclipses the larger whole, the larger whole ceases to care much about one's self. Many, if not most, mental health problems could perhaps be traced to this shift in perspective.

+++++

Apparently, when people are anticipating their demise, they have regrets. They do not so much express regret about what they have done, but about what they didn't do. This is essentially expressing regret about certain intentions unfulfilled. In everyone's life, there are trivial intentions. But there may also have been highly vital intentions that may have gone unfulfilled. If you married the wrong person, you may have had an intention to do something to fix that. If your work life turned out to be not nearly what you intended, you may have had some intentions about what you ought to do about that. If you seem to have lived but not the life (or the experiences) you intended, you may end up with a "bucket list" that you intended to fulfill, but didn't. You should have had a better life (whatever that means to you), you should have kissed your partner more (whatever that means to you), but you didn't. But at that point it may be too late. Actually, at any point in your life, it may have been too late. That's the popular song theme about "the one that got away."

Intentions are like fresh fruit. So appetizingly imagined, but so quickly spoiled if not devoured. The French have one kind of metaphor about arriving too quickly with regret, too late for one's intentions. It is this: *"esprit de l'escalier."* It means that the witty retort that could have made you the life of the party comes to you as you are going down the stairs away from the gathering. Intentions are like that. You intended to make a stunning comment at the gathering, but it comes to you too late. If you miss saying just the right thing to the person you wanted to marry, the right thing may occur to you too late. If you interview for a position but fail at a critical juncture, you may have had this feeling about what you didn't say, or didn't do.

Some people fulfill their intentions, and there are others who don't. We may think that there is some mystical difference between those who do and those who don't. But that's not it. What the difference is can be measured. For example, and in basis: If a person does not follow-through on their intentions, *it is because they have a habit of not doing so.* Competence at anything takes time and designated practice. The second reason is not quite so obvious. Those people who follow-through on their intentions do so *because they feel it is necessary (for them) to do so.* So it is a combination of competence and internal necessity that is the difference. Becoming competent at something so vital requires small steps that add up to larger steps, and then larger steps that add up to good intentions fulfilled.

Some readers of this book will come away with much of value to them in crafting their lives. Others may not see any value (for themselves). Some people are simply better readers over time than others. And some people may be driven by the necessity for learning what they need to learn, as above. If you don't *need* to know what may be herein for you, you won't. And if you are not a competent enough reader to co-author this book to your everlasting benefit, you cannot do so.

So...what is your intention? And do you have what it takes to fulfill it? Or have you not been practicing your intentions?

+++++

Procrastination is not assumed to be a serious disease in America. That may be because everyone is guilty of procrastinating at one time or another. If everyone does it, it must be okay to do it. Procrastination is in its simplest form merely putting off until "tomorrow" what needs to be done today. This could be due to an inability to figure out what needs to be done today. Or, it could be due to a lack of conscience, or a sense of duty or obligation. But, most likely, it could be due to the fact that putting off tasks that one doesn't really feel like doing is more or less normative in our culture. Even a 2-3 year-old child knows how to procrastinate. Where are they getting this – from the media or from their parents and/or siblings? By the time they are teenagers, they will be experts at procrastinating because it is normative.

Putting off one's intentions until tomorrow may be harmless. But, as we all know, tomorrow never comes. What can be put off until tomorrow may turn out to be something we'll attend to whenever we "get around to it." It has often been observed by minds superior to ours that most things that could happen never do. When the whole class (in school) is late with an assignment, most school-age youngsters don't feel guilty. They feel relieved. That's the way normative things work. If "everybody" is doing something (or, in this case, *not* doing something), one can easily justify his or her behavior on the basis of how widespread that behavior is. One's unfulfilled intentions may be inconsequential at the level of a whole society. But when large numbers follow the norm, it could be disastrous. No single snowflake in an avalanche ever feels responsible, as Lec once quipped. So it may also be a way of avoiding responsibility, which is increasingly endemic in our society. Middle managers in business or government avoid personal responsibility by creating "teams." Top executives avoid personal responsibility by doing (or not doing) what is being done by the top executives they know – or read about because their recipes are contained in best-sellers. A hero in combat is simply the person who follows his or her sense of duty, and not the level of procrastination that the majority seem to exhibit (in the sense of "That's not my job. Let someone else do it"). It is a sense of duty to oneself and to others that is missing. There are risks involved in being courageous (or dutiful). Such a sense of "duty" is not normative. One avoids it by joining the majority. Failing one's intentions has become the norm. Fulfilling one's duty earns one being ridiculed by one's peers. People at work feel comfortable surfing the web and shopping on company time. They are supplied a computer and get paid for doing this. That must make sense to some hyper-liberal economist. In huge bureaucracies, like the government, it takes three people to do the work that could be done by one person. That makes sense only if it is normative. Most people are mediocre, but not by intention.

We live in a world in which where we are encouraged to do only what we want to do. Who ever intended to have such a world? Is the ideal world one of not having any intentions beyond immediate stimulations? Is failing to fulfill one's chosen intentions a path to salvation? Oscar Wilde observed that

>*"Everything popular is wrong."*

Certainly he didn't mean to imply that everything that is *not* popular is right. He was far smarter than that. In a liberal democracy we live by what we hope to be popular opinion. Where does that lead us? What *did* Wilde intend to provoke by his pithy remark? If you were the most popular kid on your block or in your school, then it is unlikely you will ever make a worthy contribution to your family or the organization you work for. What is it that makes an intention *worthy*? Criminals and politicians often carry out their intentions. Is that what makes them worthy of the attention of the news-gatherers?

+++++

Intentions are personal and subjective. Their consequences, if carried out in the larger social world are often treated as more objective. An intention, whether carried out or not, has real and measurable consequences. What makes our subject so difficult to access but so consequential is this subjective <–> objective divide. In our pop culture, we are inclined to think that the nature of the society influences the nature of the person in it. It seems far more difficult to think about how a person and what she thinks or does will influence the society.

But it does. If those ways of thinking and doing are the way they are because they are normative, then that signals the destiny of our civilization. Social revolutions are no longer in fashion. Demonstrations seem to be. There are professional demonstrators who can be hired for a small price. If you think more independently, you run the risk of being ostracized. If you think normatively, you will feel more secure, but your group or society will be weighted in the direction it is going – which may be a greater risk.

So your intentions – anyone's intentions – are far more consequential than we might be led to suspect. We have no way of making any one person's intentions legal or illegal. And we live in a modern legalistic, not a moral, society. If your intentions are not ruled by your conscience, their may be trouble ahead. There is an interesting stanza in the poet Robert Burns' poem *To Robert Graham:*

> *"When nature her great masterpiece design'd,*
> *And fram'd her last, best work, the human mind,*
> *Her eye intent on all the mazy plan,*
> *She form'd of various stuff various Man."*

"Mazy" here means "like a maze." People's minds functions like a maze – traversable (if at all) only by that person. People (particularly modern people, whom Burns foresaw) are perverse. They are perverse only to those who view them objectively. But the observer is similarly perverse. Thus when we think about intention, we are stuck with a perverse mind explaining a perverse mind.

How we explain things determines the flavor of our intentions. And we *can* explain anything we want to talk about. (Do you, in your experience, need convincing?) Cultures vary because they explain things differently. People vary because they explain things the way their peers do, and sometimes only the idiosyncratic way they do. A person who is too far from the norm is often labeled "crazy." But it is possible that it is the norm that is crazy (as Szasz argued). We cannot know which. But we can readily explain that it is the nonconformist who is "crazy," since that's the way the people in our social circles explain it. We are formed of various stuff. Therefore our collective interpretations of what is going on may take us down the wrong path in the maze. Individually we may take the wrong path. Collectively we may take the wrong path.

When we acknowledge that people have intentions, what we are really saying is that those intentions may be right or wrong – right or wrong for the person, and right or wrong for the group, the organization, or the larger society. It is in this sense that it makes sense to study the impact of intention in our lives.

In *Troilus and Criseyde* (1629), Chaucer wrote that intention is all. What he probably meant by this is that intention precedes action, and therefore that the consequences actually come from one's intentions. If the consequences are efficacious (good for the individual, good for the larger whole), then no matter the intention.

If, however, the consequences are not efficacious, then there may have been something wrong with the intention. If there is a need for charity, there have to be people who need it in the eyes of those who provide it. You have to have rich people in order to have poor people. What is it about our way of explaining things that makes this so? Was this someone's intention? Or do the things that happen to us individually or collectively have to be brought about by someone's intentions in the past?

+++++

Are random happenings intentional? In our modern, scientific world, we are inclined to believe that everything must have a cause. What is the cause of an "accident"? Someone's intention, or someone's inattention?

And, in no sense by the way, what does attention have to do with intention? If we pay attention to whatever happens to come along, then we are not doing triage with respect to our intentions because we don't have any. If we don't pay attention to what is going on, we may be crippling our intentions because of the role that random happenings may have when we are trying to fulfill our intentions.

People who "fall" in love seem to fulfill their marital intentions in general around 50% of the time. Why is that? People who have intentions regarding their working lives seem to fail more often than they succeed. Why is that? People who die before intended often feel cheated. Why is that? On the other hand, whoever intends to die, or to fail at life? If our intentions are not life-giving, what are they for?

These are the kinds of delicious issues that we will tackle in the pages ahead.

It is, indeed, a complicated and convoluted subject. What we will be doing in this book is pulling the entrails of the pieces out until we can see how they influence each other. At least, that will be my intention. If you like the puzzling dilemmas that have become so much a part of your life, what will be your intention?

2 Intention: the Inside Story

The "inside story" (which is our beginning) is what goes on privately within a person who has an intention, and does or does not act on or talk about it. It is subjective because one's intentions don't become public until he or she acts on them. If you don't write down your New Year's resolutions (or any intentions) or talk about them with others, they remain unknown to anyone but you. Today we may have an intention to say or do something. Tomorrow we may not harbor that same intention. If we have not made it public, no one but you will be impacted by it. It's as if it never existed. But it existed for you if no one else, and that is the "inside story" we want to explore in this chapter.

It is important to understand that any person's intentions are private and inaccessible to anyone else unless that person talks to others about them, or otherwise makes them public by declaration or by action. If you see someone rushing to the restroom, you might deduce that their intention has to do with being inside the restroom. If you see someone speeding on the highway or side street, you might deduce that their intention lies somewhere in the exhilaration they feel in speeding. Or even that they might be inebriated. If you see your sexual partner kissing someone else, you might deduce that something is amiss between the two of you, or with the interloper. Your deduction might be right. Or it might be wrong. It remains an interpretation – an attempt to make sense of something by attributing it to what you believe to be that person's intentions.

But how can you make sense of something that was unlikely to have been intended? If a person is involved in an accident, or falls sick or dies, could any of those have been intended? Before we got rid of our gods as not being corporeal in our modern world (because we believe that *we* are), we could attribute certain otherwise inexplicable happenings to them. The way we see things in our worlds, there has to be some kind of intention, or *cause*. We have trouble understanding anything until we can attribute it to *some* cause. As we drifted into secularism, people's intentions came to be the source, the cause, of what happened. (Except in courts of law, where the accused in the West had to have a "motive" which caused her to do what she did beyond her control. Japanese law still seeks intention.)

So as an idea about how things happen in our social world, intention has had a history. In a moralistic society, it still does. Our own cultural evolution is being eclipsed by scientism, which does not want to deal with anything as subjective as intention. If you hurt someone's feelings, it matters little whether or not you *intended* to hurt that person's feelings. If you cheated on your partner, but did not intend to, does that change anything? Pharmaceutical firms (and other marketers) intend to deceive us about their products in order to separate us from our money. We know this. But because it is so ubiquitous in our lives, we no longer pay it heed. *Caveat emptor* is not a contemporary injunction. At least half of the people who get married in the U.S. are lying about their commitment. Do they do this intentionally, or only because in our world they are free to change their minds and thus their intentions?

It is those kinds of questions, and the questions or issues of concern to you personally or professionally that we will want to explore in this chapter. What we will want to focus on is how a person's intentions bear upon his life, and upon what happens if that person does or does not act upon her intentions.

The more deeply you think about this stuff, the more your reading about it will pay off for you.

+++++

You did not appear on this planet as a result of any of your own intentions. You are the product of someone else's intentions. Your first realization might have been that their intentions did not include having a petulant child or a rebellious adolescent. They must have had other, shorter-sighted, intentions, if they had any at all. If you got here by others' intentions, and most of what happens to you from birth on for some years doesn't come about by your intentions, how come you are who you are? Are you early on more what other people intend or what you intend? If you live primarily by others' intentions, where would your own intentions come from? If you are a victim of your parents' intentions, and then become a victim of your peers' intentions as an adolescent, when do you begin to have intentions of your own? And would they – could they – be of higher quality than the ones you have been exposed to?

Research can be taken to suggest that the further out your intentions extend, the more likely you are to fulfill them. In other words, if your New Year's resolutions were for your life rather than the calendar year, the more likely it would be that you would actually follow them. In our culture, we don't plan our lives, we plan our weekend festivities. Our vacations are better markers of our lives than are our intentions. It isn't that your life is planned along the lines of your intentions for it. It is that we more universally acquiesce to what happens to us along the way as more important. The customs in one's social circles may be more influential than any intentions one may have.

The social critic and philosopher E. M. Cioran made this observation:

> *The most important decision you make in your life is who to have as parents.*

Literally, it is readily apparent that no newborn makes that decision. So Cioran must have been tempting us with a metaphor. Our "parents" are throughout life simply those who most influence the way we think and feel and act. If you grew up in an American Indian tribe, your parents would have been all of the people in the tribe who were older than you were. So, like most other words, parent is a metaphor. Whether we read their books or watch our celebrities on the screen, or converse with them at work or play, they may be the people who most influence the person we are becoming throughout our lives. We are either influencing them (given the strength of our intentions), or they are influencing us. Your parent may be in part an ancient philosopher. Or your parent may be a contemporary celebrity – a sports star, a movie star, a politician – most probably anyone who is well known. As Daniel Boorstin said (in *The Image*), "people are well-known for their well-knownness." And the more well-known they are, the more likely we are to claim them as friends, or to be one of their fans. An every day gossip circle evolves its own hierarchy of influence. We may not want to be like one or more of our influencers, but we may. You can tell where the influence comes from simply by observing who is more often influenced by whom.

What this might suggest to you is that the people who you permit to influence you the most are in direct competition with your most cherished intentions. If you imagine your parent would not approve of your intentions, but would approve of his or her influence over you, your intentions may be eclipsed.

The popular culture influences and channels people's intentions. You are unlikely to have intentions that are not popular. And, as an outside influence, *the influence of the pop culture, in conjunction with your personal influencers, may nullify any fledgling intentions you might have.* In the modern world, we may be inclined to think that we control our own lives far more than we actually do. For example, if a young person is ridiculed for her outfit at school once or twice, she may intentionally change the way she dresses to be more like her peers. If your boss at work criticizes your initiatives once or twice, you may be inclined to keep your intentions to yourself and not make them public. Your own spouse may be disinclined to entertain your intentions for bettering the relationship. An intention that is not sanctioned by the pop culture is unlikely to have a warm welcome, even amongst friends.

Is your intention, acted upon, consistent with how people see you? If so, it might be acceptable. If not, you are likely to run up against resistance of one sort or another. So it makes a difference how accurately you *read* those other people who will be implicated in your actions. If you misread them, they might be resistant – rather than to facilitate – your intentions. That's why Republican speakers try to fill their audience with Republicans, and Democrats try to fill their audience with Democrats. At least, they might get the benefit of the doubt. A professor, these days, is faced with a belligerent audience of people who are there to resist any attempt the professor makes to teach them anything new. They already know everything they need to know, including their competence at disagreeing with any person who is flying colors they don't happen to believe in. They feel it is their prerogative to judge. Anything beyond what they already know is suspect. In our world, people don't do such wondering as might lead to questions. They have opinions that are fixed because *they* are. Don't go into a regular church gathering to try to convince people that they should be skeptics. It's much like the old adage: *"Don't try to kiss a person who is leaning away from you."* The tricky thing is that if you don't go public with your intentions amenable to being convinced otherwise, it's likely they won't either. If a person you intended to seduce into your way of thinking doesn't want to go there, your powers of persuasion may be inadequate.

+++++

Let's say that you have good intentions, and you want to fulfill them in the larger social world – perhaps not too far-fetched. This still leaves you with three dilemmas:

1. What makes you think your intentions may be considered good ones by other people? A boss may intend that her subordinates should work smarter because it is in their best interests to do so. But if those subordinates don't like their boss,

or simply think that becoming "smarter" might be hard work, they may be likely to interpret her good intentions as being bad for them.

2. The distance between having good intentions and carrying them out in the real world can be beyond the capabilities of the person who has the intentions. It's far easier to think them up than it is to carry them out. If they involve only the person who has them (like a New Year's resolution), it is theoretically possible for everyone. The more others involved, and the more diverse they are, the more difficult the task will be. In our world, we are not brought up to deal with impediments to our intentions. So most people either give up trying, or give up having any public intentions at all.

3. This leaves us with the central conundrum: what happens when you have what you believe to be good intentions, but for some reason you do not carry them out?

First, what makes an intention a *good* intention? If it serves the *worthiest* purposes of the intender, we could say it is a good intention. If it serves well the best self-interests of his or her larger social circles, then we might say it is good. If it serves well the destiny of the society, then it is a good intention. *The measure is in the consequences, not in the intention.* And all of this assumes that such a good intention was effectively fulfilled, which is not always the case. It is a *bad* intention which has bad consequences for any or all of the people affected by it.

Second, there is the issue (to be considered carefully) of the competence of the person to carry out his or her good intentions. People vary greatly on this score. There are people who have few intentions – or no intentions. They live their lives as victims, being passively accommodating to whatever happens to them. But if a person has a purpose or purposes in life, then they will serve those intentions (or not) depending upon how capable they may be to fulfill them. A worthy purpose calls for worthy intentions. What confounds people is having worthy intentions for an unworthy purpose, or having unworthy intentions for a worthy purpose. (You may want to think about this. Most people seem unable to do so.) And they may not be aware of how critical good intentions are even in the most casual conversation. Everything results from the conversations that a person has *with herself* or with others.

Third, what happens if a person has intentions, but for one reason or another fails to carry them out? The first thing to notice is that a person who habitually has good intentions but fails to carry them out is essentially lying to themselves. It may seem trivial because "everyone" does it. But it has its negative consequences for the person nonetheless. There are three:

1. Lying to oneself in this way makes it easier for the person to lie to themselves about other matters. And it makes it easier for this person to lie to *others* about anything, especially what is indispensable to their relationship. For example, love is about the other person, not oneself. So if a person lies in order to avoid intimacy, they may have been lying at the outset, or in the present. One is either obligated to fulfill a promise, or they are not. Love and affection, which may have been the original promise (spoken or implied) fades away over time

because there was no real commitment to the vows they exchanged. They probably intended well. But years of denying their intentions can lead to trivializing them.

2. When intentions are not acted upon, they become part of the dendrites of life. They are discarded and end up in the mind's trash dump. Like calories for which there is no need, they become a part of the obesity of the person's mind. This leaves a person sluggish and largely unenthusiastic about life. According to the pop culture, we are supposed to be comfortable and at ease at all times. Having an intention is disruptive to the status quo. After a while, carrying out an intention looms so disruptive to one's comfort zone that we cease to do so. We *have* to go to work. We *choose* to go to the party. It becomes easier to entertain intentions that have no bearing on our destinies. Except we may pretend we're having "fun" because we're supposed to have fun when mixing with others. We go to the rock concert to have fun. That's an intention. We carry it out because we want to be a part of whatever the fans do. We feel indispensable without ever having a conscious intention of doing so. That's what is behind the observation that we are herd animals. We do whatever "everybody" in our presence is doing. That way we neither have to have intentions of our own and thus we don't have to feel guilty about not carrying them out.

3. Given that we live out our lives looking in the rear-view mirror, there comes a time when people look back at their lives and feel some sense of *regret*. They don't so much regret what they have done. They regret what they intended to do, but didn't do. Many older people feel sad about their lives, not

because of what they did, but because they had good intentions that they did not fulfill. Most people, sooner or later, get married. Apparently they do so simply because that is what is done. The complaint is, "How did I get *here*?" (And more than half seem to decide there is no good answer, so they get out of there into a similar there.) Second marriages on average do not last the same normative 8-9 years as the first one. There is no "human nature" at work here. There is only the working of the pop culture. We are imperfect people attempting to achieve perfection in the imperfect world we have made. Sad? Or just ironic?

We seem to want the freedom to have our own intentions. But we don't want the responsibility of carrying them out. Maybe *intention* has to do not with what we intend but what we desire. The good comes not from the good intention, but from the excellence of the commitment. *Character comes from commitment and its consequences, not from good intentions.*

+++++

Most Christians perhaps have good intentions. But they don't always behave as if they did.

Most Muslims perhaps have good intentions. But they don't always behave as if they did.

Most Buddhists (and so on down through the splintering sects) perhaps have good intentions. But they don't always behave as if they did.

Most of us average folk probably have good intentions. But if there were a road to hell, we are paving it and it is all downhill. Individual conscience evaporated as quickly as did the god who was supposed to be our savior.

Since there is no one to reward us for being good, or to punish us for being bad, we just do what we do with or without intending, and hope for the best. Many of those who play war games abhor war. To fail to carry out our good intentions make of us something like hypocrites with respect to ourselves. We know how to politick. We know how to say one thing that we think puts us in good light, but do another. Do the rich and powerful have good intentions? How would we know? Since hypocrisy is the tie that binds us, and we cannot trust *ourselves* to do the right thing, we trust our experts and our celebrities. But it turns out that they, too, see no higher goals in life but their own – which usually have to do with money or with advantage. It is a small thing, an intention. But it can have huge social consequences. Our parents lied to us, our teachers lied to us, our pastors lie to us, our friends lie to us for their advantage, and we lie to ourselves for what we take to be our advantage. We don't do it well. We just do it. We try to impress others by decorating ourselves with our clothes, our makeup, and our coiffures. It works...for a day or so. People who fall in love are rarely honest with one another. People who fall in love – or have some other need to believe – do not criticize and judge one another when they want what they want. When they get what they want, it seems to come with a license to judge one another. Love cannot survive in a manipulative relationship – which more and more of them seem to be. A person who comes with the right material for a lasting relationship seems to be fading into the morass. In a phony society, it is usually disadvantageous not to be phony.

To consider just the Christians: We want some god to tell us what we should do. But we don't do what they admonish. The gods gave up and left us to our own waywardness. So we're stuck for any direction except what we can provide ourselves. At this, we do not do very well, it seems.

And this may not have been our intention.

In a world of hyper-individualism, of indulgence and permissiveness, we relish being the center of the universe. But we may harvest what we sow.

Certainly if it is our intention to treat people as if they are in our lives solely for the use that we can make of them, they will come to treat us in the same way. Did we intend for our society to turn out to be as narcissistic as it seems to be (e.g., the "Selfie")? Or did it just happen? Most social or cultural movements cannot be traced to a single source. They just seem to happen, in spite of our intentions (if, indeed, they are contrary to our intentions). But if things can happen in our world without our intention (the horrors of war, for example), might there be a possibility that we can make things happen intentionally? Things that are more favorable for our lives and the destiny of our civilization? There was a time when women wore corsets, in spite of the fact that corsets were neither comfortable nor healthy. Whose intention was that? Or was the intention that of making money from a fad or fashion? Marketing is not devoted to a way of making people healthier. If it were, wouldn't we be more rather than less healthy? Does our fast-food diet have anything to do with the epidemic of obesity? Many old people are warehoused until they die. Is it intentional that they have no more than a clinical existence until they die?

Every social problem we have, just as for every personal problem we have, has what the experts call an etiology – that is, a source of the symptoms we deal with. Does a person who overdoses *intend* to die? Is it our collective intention to spend billions on addiction caused by the *choices* people make? It seems clear that there is a disconnect between our ideologies (e.g., freedom) and how those get translated by people into their consequences at the social level. We believe in abundance – but only for those who have money in abundance. Does giving children everything they want predict to a better society when they are adults? Whatever happened to connecting intentions with their consequences for all of us? Is it someone's intention to have rich people and poor people in the same society? Whose intention was it to have earthquakes or hurricanes? What did the inventor of the "smart" phone have in mind for the quality of life in our society – or for our society's destiny? (It is interesting that the first two automobiles registered in the state of Ohio crashed into each other. Whose intention was that?) People get shot by an anonymous shooter, and people get run over by an anonymous driver. People in a war zone suffer; was that your intention? There is always collateral damage where intentions are concerned. Who should be held responsible for that – the manufacturer or the product or the taxpayer?

We may be approaching the carrying capacity of our planet. If you had a child or two, was that your intention – to add to the glut?

Most things that happen to people were not *intended* to affect those people in the way that they did. That's because they were probably not intended. There are such things as random happenings. These are sometimes seen as "the law of unintended consequences." Everything that is paid attention to has consequences. The law of "unintended consequences" gets at what happens when people react to what is happening. For example, you may intend to compliment your spouse for something she did or did not do. If your spouse interprets your comments as a slur, what can you do? You can try to fix your spouse's interpretation. But this doesn't work very often. To most people most of the time, their interpretation is simply their *reality*. You can try to talk people out of their reality. But the likelihood that you can do so is mighty slim. How easy is it for other people to talk *you* out of your reality?

If it rains on the day you intended to play golf, and you don't like rain anyway, you might feel that someone or something intended to thwart your plans. You might intend to raise your children to be great adults, living good lives with other adults. But they don't automatically become adults. That requires some effort and some good mentoring. Many people who become parents are themselves not adults. For one reason or another – poor parenting, poor choices of influential peers, sloth, too permissive a pop culture – they were stultified in the growth that was needed. If they are not made accountable, it is unlikely that they will be accountable. If their aims in life are comfort and joy, it is unlikely that they will have a worthy purpose for their own lives. If they think in terms of entitlements and not obligations (even to themselves), they are likely to have problems later on. An adult knows that it is the choices they make today that predict to the lives they will have in the future. Adolescents of any age may refuse to feel responsible for the lives they have as a result of the choices they have made.

For increasing numbers of people, it seems, the intentions they may have are of the moment and not about their future. They change their intentions to fit the circumstances of the moment (as they interpret those circumstances). The fact that people's intentions are increasingly short-term, almost exclusively self-serving and otherwise arbitrary, may belong to the law of unintended consequences. People may be happy with their indulgences (many of which they will later regret). But they may also be channeling the larger society down a slippery slope to its doom. In a paradoxical way, our hyper-individualism (that is, when everyone has a "right" to their own opinion, based on nothing but their intentions of the moment, without regard for the larger whole) there is trouble brewing ahead. One sees this in marriages and other relationships, in organizations, in the absence of a treasured community and the concomitance of the experienced irrelevance of one's own life, and in the pursuit of happiness with third-party payers. Our nest is the larger whole. We are fouling our own nest. Is that anyone's intention?

+++++

There is a world of difference between happiness and meaning. Happiness is thought to be something from outside oneself that "causes" one to be happy...or not. Meaning doesn't directly cause anything. It has little to do with the vicissitudes of life. It comes from making choices – about what to imbibe of the outside world and how to create the person one would be (Epictetus frames this best). If you don't choose what you would be in your life, the pop culture and your friends will do it according to whatever is in fashion at the time. The risk you take on that path is that of becoming an automaton. The risk you take in choosing is alienation. Most people in our age don't want to deal with other people who determine their own path. They want to know and hang out with other people who confirm that *they* are on the right path. A person who chooses his or her own path is a disconfirmation to the rest of us of their own lives and its waywardness. To live a meaningful life takes one outside of the puddle of sameness. It makes you less like other people and more like yourself. One may not find happiness there, if happiness is to be had in being a fan of movie or sports celebrities. Those celebrities we worship may have lots of hangers-on. But they have little life of their own. If you can't find happiness in solitude, you will have to pursue it in a crowd. That was probably not your intention when you first started thinking about the part you needed to play in crafting your own life. It all depends, as the social philosopher Cioran said, on who you choose as your parents – the people whose voices you permit to influence you and your life's direction. In other words, it makes a great deal of difference who you hang out with – directly or indirectly.

If that is not your intention, then you probably won't have one of your own. You will take your intentions off the shelves of the pop culture.

If you have chosen intentions and they are indeed your own, and if you have what it takes to carry them out, you might be labeled a sociopath – for good or for ill. Minimally you will be labeled a nonconformist. Has there ever been in human history a leader who was a conformist?

That's part of the inside story. There's also of course an outside story. We will continue that story in the next chapter, if you make that your intention....

3 Intention: the Inside <--> Outside Story

What a person does about his or her intentions will indeed affect that person in vital ways we have already discussed. If those intentions are acted upon they will also indeed affect others – and, ultimately, the destiny of the society in which they are enacted. One's subjective world is the most influential world for the person who lives by it. Those subjective worlds impact the world outside one's head when they are acted-upon. And nowhere is this more crucial than when one carries out his or her intentions. An intention not acted upon impacts no one except the person who harbors it. An intention acted upon impacts others in myriad, often unpredictable ways. Churchill had an intention. Many people died as a result of how he acted upon his intention. Hitler had an intention, as did Mao and Stalin. Those who survived are today British or American and not German, Chinese, or Russian. Hitler had an intention. Millions died in his camps who had not intended to. Queen Elizabeth had an intention. The royal family receives more publicity than do Great Britain's elected politicians. Moses had an intention, which came as a command from *his* god. So far, so good...for *his* people. Maybe not so good for other people and *their* gods.

Acted upon, the intentions of powerful or influential people (e.g., celebrities) can have widespread and even lasting impact. And there will always be unintended consequences. Darwin didn't intend to impact the educational establishment or the popular culture of America. But his beliefs have, in much the same way that

Catholicism has. One may intend for his influence to be
local. But it sometimes turns out that the world changes
as a result. There has perhaps been as much written
and popularized in films, etc. about Don Quixote as
about Darwin (which in itself is enormous). But Darwin's
impact fit the times. Quixote's impact is more on the
imagination and the assumptions made in the West just
about living. Darwin dealt with stuff. Quixote's appeal is
to people who wonder what it might be like to live in an
ideal (not a literal) world. In that, he had a more modern
spokesperson in the form of Goethe, who advised:

> *"You should love people not for what they
> are, but for what they could be."*

What that might mean to us moderns is that loving
people for what they are tends to keep them as they
are. If you love them for what they could or should be,
some may continue to grow in that direction. Dulcinea is
satisfied with her life as a peasant. But to Quixote, she is
his princess, his paramour. To fall in love, you must see
your target as perfect, as ideal. We fall out of love when
the ideal fades under the impact of the everydayness of
things. We may revere beauty in our culture, but the
average tenure of a first marriage in our world is less than
9 years. It is only the literal that is reachable. The ideal
requires an imagination. Darwin was wildly imaginative.
But he sought the answer and not the wonder. Quixote
sought the wonder (even Pancho did not join him there
entirely). Quixote offered a way to live a richer life. Darwin
offers only a way to know the answers. Perhaps this lies
at the heart of our contemporary malaise? Isn't that one
interpretation of Einstein's famous statement?

> *"Imagination is more important than facts."*

And yet we send our children to school generally to give up their indispensable imaginations and gain some irrelevant facts.

+++++

Thus the first thing to contemplate in our exploration of *intention* in our personal lives and the life of our culture is that there are intentions that are malignant (potentially bad for us) and intentions that are beneficent (potentially good for us). Knowing which is which requires having a purpose for one's life. People who have no particular purpose for their lives find it hard to distinguish the one kind of intention from the other. Our pop culture may be telling them that the purpose of life is to be comfortable and to have "fun." Any serious intention carries with it the responsibility for carrying it out. Most people grow up in our permissive society inclined to avoid such personal responsibility. Having a purpose in life can be uncomfortable and not particularly fun at times. To compete in the next Olympics, for example, may require hours in exercise to a few minutes on the slopes or in the pool. Sports *fans* may expend as much energy as do the well-honed players on the field. Being in a crowd of fans is fun in a way that practicing 10 hours a day may not be. If it's frigid, it may not even be comfortable to be a fan in the stands. But it is heroic and good for conversational topics for days afterward. Fanship has its own rewards. It's easier and far less risky to be a fan of some performer (politics or pop culture) than to do what has to be done when you could actually fail at it.

The point was, and is, that people who don't have a worthy purpose in life (beyond fanship or celebrity worship) find it very difficult – sometimes impossible – to tell the difference between intentions that may be good for them and intentions that may be bad for them. In this, the pop culture is not their friend. The pop culture has no conscience. Their friends and acquaintances may not be the ones they need – just the ones that readily justify their waywardness. Peer pressure or peer corroboration has no conscience. Having a purpose to which a person is committed brings with it a certain responsibility. That may be a core reason for why so many people avoid it. Many people seem to be able to harbor and even carry out certain short-term intentions. Long-term intentions (or purposes) might be entertained. But they are rarely carried out. The more difficult the task of carrying out an intention seems to a person, the less likely she is to undertake and persist in the task. If an intention looms as a threat to one's identity, it is also unlikely to be undertaken. As bad as they may sometimes report them to be, people's circumstances in life as practiced becomes their status quo. And any threat to one's status quo or habituated lifestyle is apt to be rejected. One's habits are likely to be more potent than one's intentions in life. That's why adults may report dissatisfaction with their lives, but never get serious about doing something positive about them. They may intend to (when they get around to it). But one's intentions about one's life are likely to flame out before one does anything about them. The struggle envisioned for actually getting involved in carrying out any intention that portends changing oneself is likely to be stillborn. All intentions are much easier to talk about than to carry out, even if one is talking only to oneself.

+++++

Don Marquis (1878-1937) once quipped:

> *"Ours is a world where people don't know what they want and are willing to go through hell to get it."*

We may know what we want today or even tomorrow. And usually those wants are material, not spiritual. What most people want is to get through the work day (or the leisure day) with as much comfort and security as possible, with the hope that tomorrow will bring more rewards and ease of life than yesterday. We have a vague sense of our comfort zones. Our hope is that they don't get disrupted by forces outside ourselves. We assiduously avoid disrupting them ourselves. A tasty meal may outweigh a tasty idea any day. There are always diversions on sale (television, X-box, etc.) for those who would otherwise not know how to kill the time on their hands until time kills them.

The "...willing to go though hell to get it..." is interesting. People who are not devoted to their own purposes in life adapt to whatever comes their way. This is probably what Marquis meant by "hell." It is a hellish life, this life without purpose. People who choose their purpose in life work at it. What happens on their path to their purpose is not any "hell," but merely something to be dealt with in order to stay on or return to the path to their purpose. If they need strength, the exercises they must undertake and endure are not what the purposeless imagine them to be. They are even enjoyable if they bring one's purpose clearer into view. Otherwise, exercise and diet appear to be anathema to the "good" life – which is one's comfort zone writ large.

Some people have come across Epictetus's dictum for living:

"First, say to yourself what you would be; then do what you have to do."

How much simpler could a recipe for the art of living be? In terms of professing – to ourselves and others – such an intention or purpose, we might think of ourselves as virtuous. But: Immersed as we are in our pop culture, we are inclined to assume that the saying itself is going to do it for us individually. It will not. The part about doing what has to be done to achieve such an end inhibits most people. We believe fervidly in our "rights" and our entitlements. We "deserve" them. But where is it written that we must earn them? There are few if any popular songs about earning them. Wishing upon a star is supposed to be enough. So we talk a lot about our intentions, our purposes. But our pop culture doesn't really focus on the part about doing what we have to do to fulfill our hopes and dreams. It may be costly (in many ways), but all you have to do to live "happily ever after" is get married. Finding the leader who will save us from ourselves is no more than a human "right" – right?

Gandhi said:

"A small body of determined spirits fired by an unquenchable faith in their mission can alter the course of history."

He believed that. You can know that he *really* believed that because he did just that.

Most people have intentions (fleetingly perhaps) at odd moments of most of their everyday lives.

There is beyond the person the whole matter of how good one's intentions are for the larger whole – from a friendship or a marriage to an organization to a community to a civilization. This deserves pondering.

When a baby is learning how to walk, she has no intention of getting somewhere – of anywhere in particular in the house – by walking. Her destination may only be the approval of her onlookers. In learning how to walk she creates more problems for her parents or caregivers. She breaks things, gets into things she oughtn't to get into. So is learning how to walk an unmitigated good thing? Not always. It comes about intentionally, with much encouragement. But it changes the family dynamic.

Later, in her earliest school experiences, she may want a classmate to be her "best friend." But will she choose a peer who is good for her, or for her future? Not necessarily. It's the friend she wants, not the consequences. This kind of shortsightedness often accompanies youngsters into their teens and even beyond. People have short-term intentions. But they rarely think through the likely consequences of their short-term wants or intentions (or the absence of these).

By the time she's ready to move on from preschool, the influences that have guided her at home begin to shrink and the influences of her ever-expanding social circle of peers increase. She is now a fledgling person in her larger world. At the same time, she begins to have intentions that seem to her to be her own. She will become a person of her own in the company of her pseudo-parents: what her "friends" tell her, what she observes in her social environment (like TV) tell her, and what she reads tell her. She struggles in the cacophony of the day's fashions. She wants to be herself, but she also wants to fit in, by how she thinks, how she talks, and how she does what she does. She learns acceptance by some peers, and rejection by others. She didn't intend to wear the wrong outfit to school or to like a subject she wasn't supposed to like (according to her peers). Conflicts abound as she tries to find her own way but takes the ways of the groups she falls into.

Those groups or cliques are actually "epistemic communities" – to belong, she must think like they do, believe what they believe, and talk and act the way they do. She has to audition for the group or clique she wants to belong to. Rejection can be devastating. She may have been chastised at home. But it's likely she was never rejected. Who is *she*...who can be accepted or rejected by others? She may intend to be herself. But she can't be herself and still fit in. It is often a dilemma that shadows a person into adulthood, or even the rest of his or her life: how to live by one's own intentions and not the intentions of others? Not by what is in fashion, but by what might be far more beneficial in one's life, present and future? You can't both belong and follow what you believe to be your own best self-interests at the same time. You can't really belong to this or that epistemic community (like the Mafia or your social circle) by deciding your path for yourself.

So where do most people's intentions come from? They come from the people you hang out with and want to belong to. Those who have unique intentions are usually labeled sociopaths. If your aim is to kill a bunch of people you don't even know, your intention may get you removed from society but raised up in the press. Most murders occur in families, or amongst people who are known to each other. The intention is to put something lethal between you and your victims, so it may not be you but your gun that ends up being responsible.

But to go back to the far more likely story, our little girl survived family, school, and is now faced with independence. She may imagine that getting married will enable her to live happily ever after. It won't, of course. But reality hasn't a chance against custom. Who is going to tell her that is a fairy tale and that such "happiness" lives only in the imagination: her mother? That if you need another to *make* you happy you will live many years of disappointment? We're flooded by books and stories that tell us otherwise. But facts stand little chance against belief, if history is any guide. For example, people may tell a good story about peace. And they may fight to the death to attain it. Peace is boring (if you remember the story of the first man and woman on earth). It is violence and sex that sell. So will our little girl get married and take her revenge on her partner. It happens.

Chuang Tzu (centuries before A.D.) said:

> *"My greatest happiness consists precisely in doing nothing whatever that is calculated to obtain happiness."*

It has often been observed by Western philosophers and social critics that the intention to seek happiness is antithetical to happiness itself. That would make that intention the villain. It would not be the only paradox intentionality has to deal with. George Washington thought that happiness came only from fulfilling one's duty. That is what the Marines try to teach its recruits. Not all Marines are happy. Helen Keller thought that it is having a worthy purpose and pursuing that purpose that makes happiness even possible:

> ...*happiness...is not attained through self-gratification but through fidelity to a worthy purpose.*"

In an age of self-gratification and more or less no worthy purpose for living, it may be impossible to achieve happiness. Can happiness be a super-burger from the fast-food drive through? Apparently (from the expensive ads that pay for our favorite TV programs) there are many people who think so. But that would be both short-term and self-gratification. Has free speech led to a tsunami of happiness in our culture? Those for whom "free speech" has become a religion don't usually appear to be all that happy. So intentions matter. But about what do we have intentions? And what are their consequences?

+++++

We have considered the consequences of stillborn intentions. They become at least mildly toxic for the person who has them but does not follow through. That's the inside story. The inside <--> outside story is what novelists write about. All novels have their conflicts in differing intentions. A parable used to be written in order to teach us something about what our intentions *should* be. In an age being overtaken by technology, we have vignettes about which side has the technological advantage. We don't seem to care about what our intentions are. We want to be fascinated by superior firepower or superior

AI. We want winners and losers, but for technological reasons, not humanizing ones.

Parables were written for the purpose of building character. But it is not character that wins. Technological advantage does. If you are not addicted to those games, you don't know what life is really all about.

Our little girl, once married and bored with the same-old, is less likely to get addicted to war games or sports, and more likely to engage in the games that fashion magazines and television programs play with her. So her intentions are more likely about what the latest fashions are – in dress, comportment, facial expression, body appearance, and hairdos. She may not have noticed it herself, but she is more likely to talk about what married women talk about than what single women her age talk about. One way is not superior to the other way. But most people begin to think like, talk like (content), and even dress like the people they hang out with. They may even belong to the same church or country club, but they will prefer talking to those who belong to those smaller epistemic communities, the social circles of which they are members. They may not be aware of their intention to do so. But they will do so, and that turns out to be unintended but inescapable.

People don't have their identity in the larger *societal* context. They have and nurture their identities in smaller groups, where they can be known by all and seen by all. If they work in a small organization, a part of their identity will come from that culture. But when the organization is a large one – beyond mutual identity – their belongingness comes from smaller fragments of that larger whole. Although heavily influenced by the larger culture (the pop culture), they are most influenced by the people they hang out with – the smaller groups they *belong* to. We may refer to them as employees, or as citizens of the larger whole. But they will still take their cues at work from the smaller social circles they actually belong to. When they begin to feel anonymous, of not belonging, they will seek refuge in their smaller epistemic communities – the core of their mutual corroboration with others they identify with. The big boss may not like this. But they may not like her because she doesn't think like they do. People's minds may be Balkanized. But that's just the way it is.

Then there is this question of having children. It is a profound lifestyle decision. No matter what our little girl now grown up may intend, if the people she hangs out with have children, she can't fully belong unless she follows suit. If she doesn't, she will feel like an outsider of a group she wants to belong to. That is often more potent than her own intentions. There is the old proverb: "When in Rome, do as the Romans do." She will. At the end of an exhausting day, she may ask herself: "How did I ever get here?" She got there the same way she got to anyplace: By being what and doing what her peers in her social circles are and do. She might have said she would never get married, or never have children. Those were her intentions. But her intentions don't matter when there are more powerful social influences at work – which there almost always are.

+++++

Intentions are private and thus weak. What people actually do (or feel, if they talk about their feelings or beliefs) become public. The inhibiting forces are always stronger than mere intentions. They are like New Year's Resolutions. They sound good when taking a day or two off from the travails of social existence. But they fade before the onslaught of the events of the day. There is something real about what is actually going on. There is something less real about what was only thought about in private, shielded temporarily from the needs of our public lives and identities. These can only be corroborated by others if we don't want to be looked upon as insane, as not one of *us* (that is, not one of those whose group we want to belong to). People don't usually want to be pariahs. If for any reason they cannot be accepted into *any* social group, they become candidates for suicide or social violence. That was probably not their intention.

+++++

Even so, in this legalistic society we all inhabit, if we *suspect* that it was John who did some bodily harm to Mary, we seek immediately to uncover his motive (his *intention)* in doing so. We use the logic of social tools to get at his private intentions. We are always confronting this conundrum: Why did he or she do what they did? We think we know if we get to what our sleuthing has turned up. But the suspect may not know. And we have a *taboo* against admitting it was a choice. We want to believe that something *made* him or her do what they did. By the time the interrogation is over, the suspect may believe *that* judgment and begin to think that was the *motive.* The inner and the outer often have a confusing relationship. In public, we don't always say what we really think. In a war, soldiers may not really want to kill the opposing soldiers as was revealed in the grass-roots cease-fire in WWI. Maybe John didn't really *intend* the consequences of his actions. But the social sanctions trump his intentions. Anger blocks out long-range intentions. Public (legal) determination blocks out private intention under duress. Maybe the shooter didn't intend to kill or injure all of those people. But those were the consequences of his immediate intentions – whatever they were.

An intention may be responsible for some untoward action, just as it can be responsible for some normative action. But whether good or bad, an intention does not control the consequences. I can't make you happy unless you permit me to (as Eleanor Roosevelt so wisely put it). You can't make me happy unless I permit you to. The world outside of one's head doesn't function by the same logic as one's own mind does. What we can fantasize about is never the same as what we can do about our fantasies. Thirty people may have the intention of becoming President, just as 30 people may have the intention of winning the same spouse or partner. It may rain on the day you intended to play golf. Someone in front of you may have purchased the last ticket for a movie or an event you intended to attend. Your partner may decide he or she doesn't love you anymore. Try convincing a person who hates you to fall in love with you. In our imaginations, we can have it any way we want it. In the real world, we can't. In the world outside our heads, we may have to adapt to the ways of the world, or become estranged from them. The world is in no way obligated to fulfill our intentions, no matter how good or bad for us or for that world. In a world of seven or eight billion people, all having their own intentions, our personal intentions may be faced with forces of infinitely greater influence. The world follows its own logic, not ours.

+++++

It is possible that we no longer know what our intentions should be in a world we no longer really comprehend. The world is increasingly difficult to understand (because we are less capable of understanding it?). That's because the forces created by people who don't have purposeful intentions (those they are committed to fulfill) far outnumber those created by the people who do. To be seen as "with it" means that we increasingly live by exigency, and not by intention. We let what has happened or what is happening at the moment be our intention. Most people are willing to let what is on offer in the pop culture decide what their intentions as consumers should be. Our problem is not that we are overworked, but that we do not have any worthy long-term goals for our lives. When people don't have a purpose for their lives, then all information is equal. "Infotainment" fills the gaps in their days. When one is especially worth listening to, then people listen to their personal celebrities, to themselves, or to others who think and believe like they do – in that order.

+++++

When our little girl has settled in on her adulthood, she is more likely to function like an automaton than like the curious-about-everything creature she was as a little girl. (That happened fast, didn't it?). Over the years, she became a bundle of habits – of algorithms that grew out of repetition, of perspectives that filtered everything for her, without her thinking about it, and of ways of talking and doing that made her not the adult of her dreams, but of the pop culture she inherited. She became more like a fish in the water, immersed in it but not really being aware of it. She was immersed both directly and indirectly in the thinking and being and doing of her social groups.

This led to those habits – those algorithms of feelings and knowings that lived her life for her. Once those habits of seeing and doing took over, she could live out her life by not thinking about it, but just by letting this or that fashionable bit of knowledge or belief take her where it was headed.

Without seeing them for what they are, she assumed that they were the products of her own thinking, which she almost never challenged. But habits trump wishes and hopes and intentions every time. What you don't do for some worthy purpose in life becomes whatever is done for you by your habits. The universal problem in life is how to fill up one's days and years. When you live on autopilot, these become overfilled. You don't have time to think critically about your life (even if you were capable of doing so) because you are too busy to do so. You know the way to be because you are the way you are. We don't question the habits that make us look like automatons. Instead of continuing to be curious about her life and its context, our little girl now *knows* everything she needs to know to get by in her life. She doesn't question her own hours and days. She questions others' in the privacy of her own mind. She speaks from her habits, not her curiosity, not her imagination. These were eclipsed by her habits of thinking, of being, and of doing. She embraced them as short-term fixes to long-term problems – like the hopes and dreams she once had about her life.

We have seen that many if not most people have a sense of disappointment in the way their own lives turn out. That's because they are getting those off the shelf of the pop culture (and from their "friends") and are not committed to what were once their intentions in life. The first enemy to one's intentions to be encountered in life is not the world as such, but the world as one's habits make necessary how she is to be seen and understood. This is undoubtedly what Gandhi was suggesting: that if you wanted to change your world *(as it exists in your perspectives on it)*, change yourself. That changes your perspectives on the world.

As we have also seen, the world (as you may not see it) doesn't care one way or the other about your intentions. That is the world as you see it through the filters of your own habits of reckoning with it. It is the world as you see it that you have to live in. It is in the world as you know it to be (by your habits, not your intentions) that you have to forge your life. If you don't know what to make of your life, others will do this for you. There are always alternative perspectives. But to the typical adult in our pop culture, they are simply wrong. If you didn't like the movie that I liked a lot, then you are just stupid. If an orthodox Christian does not see the world the way an orthodox Muslim sees it, there is bound to be trouble.

And how *should* we see it? Neither our habits of thought or scientific "reality" can tell us. No facts can tell us what they are supposed to mean to us. What they mean to us is up to us. Our facts will always refract *our* differing cultural orientations and idiosyncratic habits of thought. Because we (people) are the ones who decide what our facts mean, they refract us more than any world. Science tells us what *their* facts are supposed to mean, just as religions do. Technologies change the world in the direction they are headed. We merely try to adapt. At least that is what we (people) may intend. We are not always successful.

What the world means to a know-it-all adult in our culture is not what the world means to a curious toddler. What the world means to a person falling in love is not what the world means to a person who is no longer loved. What the world means to a starving person is not what the world means to an overstuffed one. What the world means to a person without intentions is not what the world means to a person who is passionately pursuing his or her intentions. What snow means to an Eskimo is not what it is imagined to mean to a person who lives at the Equator.

Intention is borne as someone's fantasy. What happens when it becomes entangled in the worlds of others' intentions rarely leaves it unscathed. Intentions made public become the social porridge in which we make our way. The world as we know it (including all of the people we know) are extensions of who we are. If we can't make a life of our intentions there, those intentions die. In *Remembrance of Things Past,* Proust wrote:

> *"The bonds that unite another person to ourself exist only in our mind...Man is the creature that cannot emerge from himself, that knows his fellows only in himself...."*

If Proust is serious about the ramifications of his simple assertions – he was and we should be – what he is suggesting here is that intentions are only mind things until they are acted on. Even more counter-intuitive is the implication that they are only mind things to anyone who observes us and uses hindsight to speculate on what our intentions may have been. This is a real conundrum in modern litigation, where the issue is assumed to be "the truth." We want to know what the suspect's motive was (his or her intentions at the time of the crime). We can always ask the accused. But by the time of the trial, the accused may be confused after perhaps some hours of grilling about what his or her intentions actually were at that time in the past. What we can know is that people's memories are at best not very reliable. Even if not lying, the suspect's perspective on his or her subjective intentions will be more fiction than fact. Every otherwise sane author who writes an autobiography intends to tell a good story about their lives. The story is more important than what someone else might see as the facts. And the facts are not there to tell the story, but to make it more appealing.

Our habits, in telling our stories, are more likely to put us in the best light than to tell it like it was. And nowhere are we more likely to be subjective rather than objective than when talking about our intentions. The writer George Crabbe (1754-1832) offered these lines:

> "Habit with him was all the test of truth,
> It must be right. I've done it since my youth."

There is hardly a modern person who has not imagined carrying out some mischief or a crime just because that person felt justified in the action. But for the most part, that intention is never carried out. It ends up in the dustbin of intentions, good or bad. And "I just felt like doing it" isn't really admissible evidence in a modern court – social or legal.

People in general are believers in the truth of things. But they believe the truth of things only if it happens to be consistent with their perspective on the truth. Some people even believe that truth is the residue of knowledge and that the wisdom of their intentions is derived from the facts. In this they would be missing the perplexities of Siddhartha's (the Buddha's) dictum:

"Wisdom is not communicable."

If wisdom can't be communicated, and if wisdom is somehow related to the truth, what *can be* communicated? Obviously commercial television can be at some level. Obviously sickness can be. And obviously mediocrity does a pretty good job of getting its appeal across to millions of people. Intentions can be, if they are the ones that are already realized. Any intention to make the world and its inhabitants healthier and more concerned about its destiny is perhaps much less so. (Foundations pour millions into their advertised slogans.) Mayhem makes the news. Not much that is normative makes the news. So what is normative, even if harmful to people and their collective destiny, is not. What's communicable is whatever is believed by enough people to make it seem personally useful to them.

As the well-known poet William Butler Yeats put the contrary in *The Green Helmet and other Poems*:

> *"The fascination of what's difficult*
> *Has dried the sap out of my veins, and rent*
> *Spontaneous joy and content*
> *Out of my heart.*

4 Intention, by any Other Name

It is not even imaginable that an ordinary person could get through any ordinary day without making and probably changing their intentions from time to time. Most people are "event-driven" – that is, the exigencies of the day, from waking until sleeping, push their intentions way down in their immediate and long-range priorities. People who are "purpose-driven" do just the opposite. Their purposes, immediate and long-term take precedence over all but the lifestyle-threatening events of the day. Millions of people listen to "the news" via the media or the gossip of the day. This gives them something to think about. For those people, there is no longer anything more important to think about. Their immediate purpose is to get through the busy work day. It is often the case that the longest-range purpose they entertain in their thinking is what they intend to do once the workday is over. They anticipate relaxing. They do not anticipate with the same sense of pleasure their return to work tomorrow. Their intentions have become weaker over the years, and the events of the day increasingly displace them.

If they don't know what was on "the news" five-ten minutes ago (local or global), they are considered obsolete by those people who do. We not only synchronize our watches and clocks, we want to synchronize our minds. We want other people to pay attention to what we pay attention to, and think about it as we do. Since most people are not very good at getting other people to mind the world as they do, they do the next best thing...They mind the world the way other people do. Their intentions don't count for much in the conversational stew of the day. So they let that stew be their guide for what's important. What's important is what others are paying attention to, thinking about, talking about.

Those whose lives appear to be more interesting or dramatic than your own are those you may try to emulate – by how to look to what you can afford to buy. Those who get most often filmed and talked about in the media are more important navigational aids for one's own life than the people closest to that person. Fashions in dress and comportment go from top down to bottom up. We emulate those we hear about. We believe what our personal celebrities say and do. We disparage our elders for being obsolete. We worship our personal celebrities. Without a higher voice being heard, we fall into place according to the fashions we pay attention to. If there is no god, we have to pay attention to what is said and done by others. Unless you are a media celebrity, no one really cares what *your* intentions may be, so maybe it is best to keep them private.

The concept itself may be in the process of becoming extinct. Still, we perhaps shouldn't throw the baby out with the bathwater, a metaphor that young people don't understand. Because no one ever told them that everything human in our talk and thought is metaphorical. They fail to understand a sentence that is not literal. Therein we become literal – we are known most widely by a number like one's social security number or the ID number on your credit card. We become a nameless component of a demographic. With seven or eight billion people on this globe (or this flatland), who cares about your intentions? No camera ever captures the inexplicable. Fairy-tales can. Which is most prevalent in our culture? American Indians didn't want the camera to take their picture because (as they explained) that was messing with their souls. Since we don't have such things as what they understood (metaphorically) as their souls, we photograph everything to prove we exist in this literal world of ours. We capture ourselves in our "selfies." Where else could we have literal evidence that we exist?

+++++

In our youthful naïvete, we had intentions – for our lives, even. If we call them by another name, do they cease to exist? Can an ideal withstand the literal?

We make promises. Isn't an intention a sort of promise? Since we no longer apparently feel compelled to keep our promises, does this contribute to our indifference to our intentions? A common expression among the young is "That depends." Does snuffing out some other person's life "depend"? On what? On whether or not that now-dead person "had it coming"? On whether or not my lawyer could tell the story otherwise and thereby get me acquitted before a judge and jury? On whether or not it was my intention to do so and "I" am the only one who can stand in judgment of my intentions?

As a concept, intention probably had a moralistic meaning rather than a legalistic one. Morality had to do with keeping a person from having an intention that was not good for that person or society. In a culture like ours, your intentions are an issue only if you get caught. That's after the event rather than before the event. The differences are ubiquitous and profound.

Intentions are all future...except for the imaginary work that people do on certain events of the past to connect those dots in a way that makes a plausible and contextually-appealing story that people like to tell about their past lives. That is all rear-view.

Assuming that a *promise* might be a reasonable synonym for intention, here's the takeaway. If over time you make promises to others that you don't keep, they will cease to trust you. If you habitually make promises to yourself that you don't keep, you will over time cease to trust yourself. Every lie that you tell yourself moves you closer to being a pariah. When you become a pariah to yourself, you are courting bad trouble ahead. A promise (or an intention) is not something to be played with frivolously. If you cannot be trusted to carry out your promises, you have lied – at least you have lied to yourself. More than half the people who stand before their gods and in public make their formulaic marriage vows to one another Do they intend to fulfill their vows or not? If not, wouldn't it be better for all involved not to make them in the first place? If you don't stand by your promises, what will you stand for?

In his *Gnomologia: Adages and Proverbs* (1732), Thomas Fuller wrote:

> *"Promises may get Friends, but 'tis Performances that keep them."*

For example, promises may get lovers, but it is your reliability in fulfilling your promises that keep them. Is a promise broken a lie? Maybe to you it is not. But to those to whom you made your promise, it may be. In the real world of other people, it is often the case that their judgments outweigh yours. It is a mistake to assume that others' judgments are always in your best interests. Yet it may be as common a mistake to assume that others' judgments don't matter. You learn how to critique your own performance by considering what people whose street smarts are greater than yours think of your saying and doing.

People who don't keep their promises to others or to themselves become expert at excuses. To have excuses that work with those who matter is to live *by* one's excuses. If you can imagine that an excuse will get you off the hook for a promise you didn't really intend to keep, it becomes likely that your excuses will be the drivers of your performances. You may even get to the point where an extraordinary excuse that works for you or the larger social world in which you live will seem to you the *same thing* as the deed you promised. In the end, however, you are only duping yourself.

Abraham Lincoln averred (in his last public speech) that *"Bad promises are better broken than kept."* But what is a bad promise? Wouldn't you be better off being competent enough never to make a "bad" promise – that is, to know what you are capable of and what you are not capable of? When people practice the habit of lying to themselves, we cannot trust them to say what they mean and to mean what they say. It's akin to a kind of social death by not keeping one's promises – of being capable of lying to oneself as a result of getting away with lying to others. One advertises oneself by makeup, coiffing, dressing in certain ways, and by one's comportment. Those can always be promises en route to the slippery slope of lying to oneself, can't they?

+++++

Another concept that bears a family relationship to intention is that of *hope*. People used to invest their hopes in their deities. In modern times, people become their own deity – else what's a "selfie" for, beyond its iconography? A photograph makes it possible for one to dwell on how one appears. But photos as icons have been and will continue to be interpreted. If the interpreter is also the subject of the photograph, then the loop gets closed by an insidious circularity. There are now cameras that will allow you to change the image in the ways you would *like* to appear. In our world, there will always emerge a technological solution that actually *complicates* the problem. The icon becomes whatever the camera is capable of. Before the camera, people were who they were in a tacit relationship with other people. We no longer need other people to tell us who we are. We have our mirrors and our cameras and our secret thoughts to lie to us about who we are.

If there is a camera, people will pose for the camera. That's not who they are. They may not be sure. They're *hoping* that the mirror and the camera will tell them who they are. They may hope that they were someone else. Enter virtual reality (is there any other kind?). In some gadget, they can be anybody they want to be. That's what makes it "virtual." We moderns don't want other people to tell us who we are, or who we could or should be. We disdain any wisdom that we could not claim as our own. The more we become a one-man-band, the more we hope for something better, a better star to navigate by. So we hope in private, hoping that others who are hoping in private won't find us out. The underlying problem is that you can't be "somebody" except in relation to somebody else. We technologically destroy the central truism there ever was. But that wasn't what we were *hoping* for. Or was it?

Hope, like intention, can be very elusive. If we don't share our hopes with someone, they can be denied. If we keep our hopes private and subjective, we can always claim that our lives are exactly as we would have them be (usually with help from some alcohol or giddiness). To the extent that there are some who still believe in evidence, there seems little evidence to support that claim. People don't generally become better human beings as they get older. They placed their future in the tentacles of hope, not deed. Neither hope nor intention are good or bad until the consequences are tallied.

Hopes, like intentions, never hurt anyone outside of oneself – until they are acted upon, and then, sometimes inadvertently. If not acted upon, they become landfill (garbage of the spirit) for those who have them but hardly ever act upon them.

James Howell, around 1659, suggested that the paradox of hope is something like this:

"Who lives by hope dies fasting."

It may take some thought to get at what he is suggesting in this metaphor: that if someone lives by hope rather than action on that hope, he or she will die fasting – meaning that there is no real nutrition in hope alone. The nutrition comes from acting on one's hopes and dreams.

+++++

While pondering *intention,* it may occur to you that *wishing* is sometimes closely related. People often wish that this or that would happen, or wish that this or that had not happened. Intent is always present when wishing. We might wish to be someone other than who we are. Or we would have something in our world be other than it is. Wishing is related to intention in that way because the person wishing is wishing that something or someone – would be other than it is or they are. Cinderella may have wished for a more luxurious life. But she may also secretly might have wished that her Prince were not such a goofball that he would choose her because of her foot size.

Woody Allen once quipped:

> *"My one regret in life is that I am not someone else."*

Is it to be regretted that one is not someone else? Given the impossibility of that, of what practical good is wishing it so? A person might wish to fly like a bird. But one of our mythical characters helped others to understand that wax wings were not a good way to try. It seems that the more unlikely it is that one could fulfill one's wishes, the more one wishes. Could that have contributed to Michael Jackson's demise? Many a bride has wished for a storybook marriage, only to wish that she had a life she hadn't gotten herself into, as in the famous expression "How did I get *here*?" As Spinoza commented (speaking of hopes as well as wishes):

> *"Hope is the confusion of the desire for a thing with its probability."*

In other words, the less probable a thing is for a particular person, the more likely is his or her desire for it. We *desire* most that which is least probable...for us. It may be improbable for many reasons. A person who does not desire you in the same way you desire them is likely to increase your desire. People often desire most that which is most improbable for those people. That may be paradoxical. But it is a real driver of our thoughts, feelings, and actions. If it is improbable that you could fulfill your most rabid desires, then it may seem to you that the fault lies with the world, and not with you. Thus you cannot fail. Many people tussle with the world which they think is against them as a way of life.

An old English saying gives us this to ponder:

> *"First deserve, then desire."*

This may be taken to mean that deserving what we desire depends upon our ability to discern what we deserve before desiring it, and then equipping ourselves to deserve it. To have a great and lasting love may require you to be the kind of person who deserves it and another (better vetted?) who can bestow it. If you don't deserve a lasting love, why would you want to desire one? Philosophers have often said that the way to be happy is to desire what you already have. It's easy to see the logic in that. But the pop culture and our ubiquitous ideology of consumerism lead us to see desire as an emotional state which can only be satisfied by having something we don't have. Even billionaires seem to harbor a desire for more billions, while a person who has no shoes may desire a pair of shoes that are not worn out. Our marketing culture may incidentally confirm the wisdom of a prior choice. But it is mainly about kindling a desire for what people don't have. If you don't have "clear skin" (which in the virtual world is more appealing), you can buy it. If you don't have the right face for being "beautiful," you can buy the cosmetics needed. If you don't have the body of the model who was hired because he or she had that kind of body, you can try to buy it – but you will probably fail.

Essentially, what the old saying is trying to impart is simply that, to achieve a kind of optimum life of satisfaction, you should never desire anything you don't deserve. And, if you want to know what kind of life you deserve, look at the one you've got. If your interpersonal desires go beyond what you deserve, you are setting yourself up for troubles and disappointment. It isn't the case that you will always get what you deserve. What is the case is that if your desires exceed what you deserve because of who you are, you had better be living in fairyland, because that world is the only world in which everybody can grow up and be anything they want to be. Cinderella, our pop culture to the contrary, probably didn't deserve the prince. She didn't grow up in his world, and he didn't grow up in hers. Being royalty, he was brought up to actually deserve more than a maid who hadn't done her homework. There's trouble ahead. That's why the story ends "...and they lived happily ever after." That's the way fairy tales end. But that's not the way such coupling begins or ends in the real world. We may desire it. But, given our wayward existence, we may not deserve it. Why *do* the royals tend to marry royals? Why *do* celebrities assume they deserve more than what a commoner brings to the table? Eliza Doolittle may have been transformed by her speech. But is that who she was?

+++++

On the mundane side of things, many people have their to-do lists, for the day or the week. Those represent someone's intentions. But not always the intentions of the person to whom those tasks have been given (as in Honey-Do Lists). If these are your personal and private lists, you risk lying only to yourself. If the lists are requests imposed upon you by others who qualify, then you may risk lying to those others. People in general don't like being lied to. You may have noticed this in your parents when you were growing up.

But is a failure to do what was requested actually a lie? It seems so, if you have agreed to do what was requested. If you say you will do a thing, this assumes these two conditions: (1) that you are competent to do what you said you would do; and (2) that you are committed to doing it. Sometimes people are neither. Sometimes the real world conjures up obstacles that deter people from following through. Does this make them liars? It depends, doesn't it? How they saw the world at the outset is not how they see the world once deterred from their doing what they said they would do. In his book *Love and Lies,* Clancy Martin seems to conclude that love itself is a lie. How many are really committed to the notion that "I will love you forever" (no matter what)? Forever is a radically different time and place from the time and place of the promise.

People change their minds about things. So were they lying? *How would you know?* The professed love might last for a week or a lifetime. How could you know at the outset? A declaration is only a declaration. And, in our world, there seems to be little correlation between what people say and what they actually do. What is the shelf life of a promise?

+++++

All *plans* carry the onus of being intentions. A plan is
a kind of map for how an intention is to be carried out.
But the happenings of the real world do not necessarily
coincide with the protocols of a plan which was made
at an earlier time, in earlier circumstances. Changing
circumstances should really lead to changed people,
even more than seems to be the case. A plan is a human
artifact. The plan may not change, but the world that
happens to us is not obligated to conform to the plan.
No one is who he or she was as a baby. It's interesting
how we try to make the world conform to our plans. The
only time the world beyond us ceases changing in ways
we could not have predicted is when we die. Who we are
is a human creation. What is created can be re-created
to fit the circumstances. We may try to stop the world in
ways that affect us by claiming an identity that doesn't
change. There is no plan that is not provisional. And
there is no personal identity that is not provisional. The
problem lies in our attempts to stop time and its changes,
not with those changes. In much the same way that the
person who dies is not the person who was born, the
person who is accused of lying is not the same person as
the person who fielded the promise. Our pop psychology
may keep us from seeing this.

What gets convoluted here is an underlying need to be the
same person today that you were yesterday (a sort of pop
psych delusion given an ever-changing world encircling
you), while planning for a future in some rational way.
The problem is that tomorrow is in no way obligated to
fit your plan. Our plans are made by us, and thus carry
the assumption that we need to maintain our personal
identity no matter what happens tomorrow. If *we* changed

in a way consistent with how our circumstances change, there would be no dilemma. We would make our plans to fit the anticipated future (no matter how irrational), and not to fit our sense of an unchanging "self." Over time, many marriages are felt not to be working because of this. People strive to be who they "are," in spite of the fact that the two-person culture they share is changing all the time. If they had *planned* to change along with how familiarity and changing circumstances imperceptibly changes them, they would see that the problem is not "in" their marriage but in them. The small culture that is their relationship will invariably change, for myriad reasons. If they don't change with it, they will have problems. This is perhaps what Heraclitus meant by his assertion that "*You cannot step into the same river twice.*" The river you step into is always changing. Circumstances are always changing. Our attempts keep them unchanged in our thoughts leads us to a conflict between who we have become and how the changing world has changed us. If we attempt to see the world from an unchanging view or ourselves as having always been who we are, we are out of sync either with ourselves or with the worlds we live in. Just like the river, we are always in the process of *becoming* who we are. Our problems arise from our attempts to ignore or deny this. The world is constantly changing. We adapt. We are constantly changing. If you don't adapt, you will be at odds either with yourself or with the worlds you live in.

+++++

Every problem people confront will always have these two components: (1) one is who *they* are - which can remind us that people don't see the world as *it* is; they see the world as *they* are. People see the world as they can, and as they have to. (2) The "can" is in the possibilities given them from the cultures and subcultures they have belonged to. They have to see the world that way because it has become habitual for them to do so. The more habit-bound they are, the more they will see the world as it was yesterday, not today. The more possibilities they have been exposed to, the more likely they are to see the differences between what is going on today vs. what was going on yesterday. Language is never neutral. It will bias us in one direction or the other.

For example, in our pop culture, we can readily become hung-up in the is-ness of things. "Is" is a small word. But it can easily lead unwary people astray. We assume we are talking about the real world. We are not. We are talking about our unique interpretation of a world that is created and maintained in how we talk about things – in how we have collectively come to *explain* and understand the something we are talking about. We gloss our contribution to what we are talking about simply by assuming that we are talking about the real world, which is presumably available for everyone to see in the same way. When we use the word *is*, we assume that we are telling it like it is. Scientists talk about what "is" all the time, not realizing that theirs is but one kind of "scientific" explanation, which may or may not be superior to a mythological or any other way of explaining things. What we call pop-science may explain what it takes to make a delicious marriage. But so does religion. So do the movies. So does the friend or neighbor you may talk to. But there is not much evidence that *any* of these have made us happier with our lives in this modern world. That means that our plans as such in the modern world are not plans having efficacious outcomes, or simply were not followed, for any of the excuses we provided ourselves and others. Jeremy Bentham made this pithy comment:

> *"The infirmity of human nature renders all plans precarious in the execution in proportion as they are extensive in the design."*

This could be interpreted in different ways. But given the way Bentham thought about such things, it is likely he meant something like this: The more detailed the plan, the less likely it is to turn out the way planned.

That's because plans are conceived in a vacuum, but must be fulfilled in a real world that it more unpredictable and irrational than is the plan. You may plan to "live happily ever after." But the "infirmity of human nature" (and of the real world) makes that about a 50-50 chance of occurring. Human nature is sometimes as unpredictable as the weather.

Things happen. And those are things we can't control. We often don't know how our own perspectives will be different ten years from now.

Ambrose Bierce's writing style was not like Bentham's. In his *The Devil's Dictionary* (published around 1911), he addressed Bentham's conundrum:

> *"Plan, v.t. To bother about the best method of accomplishing an accidental result."*

His perspective is satirical, of course. He wants us to think about the rule that results occur more from accidents along the way than from any plan to achieve that result. Most lives are the result of twists and turns ("accidents") along the way than they are the result of any detailed plan.

What is not controlled cannot be predicted. And we cannot really control the machinations of the world that occur between now and some future date without our permission. Patton made an interesting comment about

> *"Plans must be simple and flexible...They should be made by the people who are going to execute them."*

His view would have been very favorable to Admiral Lord Nelson at the battle of Trafalgar. Nelson thought that his ship captains (every one of which he had mentored) were in a better position on site to make decisions than he was from afar. So he left all of their planning and execution to them. But we moderns are so enamored of the idea of "the leader" that we cling to our archaic hero worship and our belief in the superiority of hierarchy in spite of the overwhelming evidence that it is not the leader who makes the organization successful, but the organization that makes the leader successful. Most business organizations are designed hierarchically (and thus bureaucratically). The military's Special Forces are not. Many of the recurrent problems that businesses and other institutions encounter these days can be traced to this faulty thinking.

But what is even more interesting about Patton's expert observation is his notion that plans should be made by the people who are going to execute them. Custer's army might have survived if his troops had made the plans for the encounter, as was the case with the Sioux warriors.

People who make the plans in larger organizations have a vested interest in the plan's success. People on who those plans are simply imposed do not. If the people who are planning a "change," for example, do not include the people who have to execute the change, it may not happen. They have it within their power to thwart the proposed change if they don't like it.

So what might this mean to us as individuals? You might want to ponder these issues:

1. It means that if your intentions in life come from an external source (TV, the movies, books, what the people you talk to think of you), you will have less investment in executing those plans than if they had come from you. For example, you may want to be like your favorite (and rich) celebrities. If that's all you have going for you, it's unlikely your life will turn out in that direction. (If you want to be an attractive model, you may need to be attractive and to be competent as a model.)

2. It means that you engage more fully in your own plans than if they are plans that others have imposed on you. Marriage partners fantasize about what they want – not what the other person wants. So they are often at odds about what to do as a couple.

3. It means that the pop culture bits that come at you insidiously and are internalized without due thought may make you popular, but will not guarantee the consequences you imagined you had coming.

4. It means that if your aims and plans are conventional (whether intended or not) the outcomes will be conventional. You probably never

heard any of your peers say "When I grow up, I want to be mediocre." And yet, most people end up there. It requires real strength of commitment to break out of the gravity-like pull of the mediocre. Most can't muster that kind of commitment. It's either that or their fear of being different from the rest of their crowd. To be different requires... being different. The forces that channel your life are not easily conquered. It's more likely they will have their way with you, rather than the other way around.

+++++

The most common shortfall with respect to intentions is indeed what we call procrastination. For most people it occurs thus: I will get around to my personal intentions when I have taken care of the events of the day and their powerful distractions. We put off working on our intentions until everything else has been taken care of. Our intentions don't get top priority in our lives. What happens to us that might bear upon our immediate lifestyles does. The daily peregrinations of our "jobs" become an ongoing excuse for not taking time out for our own intentions. We become habituated to the events of the day. Our calendars are usually filled with things that have to be done on a schedule. We never quite schedule the time required to fulfill our own intentions. So people end up at some point in their lives when it is undeniable that they have ignored their own intentions in order to take care of things that we assume are of a higher priority. In the onrushing events of the day, many people simply loose sight of their intentions. Some refer to that condition as a "mid-life" crisis. We are made to pay for disregarding our intentions.

In his *Poor Richard's Almanack,* July 1756, Benjamin Franklin wrote:

> *"Tomorrow, every Fault is to be amended;* but
> *that Tomorrow never comes."*

How easy it is to procrastinate. But how difficult it becomes to find the time, or the place, for amending what we put off yesterday. The accumulated trash bin of our procrastinations grows beyond our abilities to do something about it. So we put off doing what needs doing. Perhaps regrettably...but perhaps not.

Oscar Wilde was famous for satirizing such human foibles as this one. In *Oscar Wilde: His Life and Wit,* Hesketh Pearson quoted him as saying:

> *"I never put off till tomorrow what I can*
> *possibly do...the day after."*

In other words, as Thomas Fuller put it: *"What may be done at any Time will be done at no Time."* In an age of waning accountability, more and more people fail to hold themselves accountable. In the typical organization, for example, it has become popular for the executives to imagine that holding everyone else accountable (except themselves) is the panacea for most of their ills.

+++++

When you die, to whom or what are you ultimately accountable? The answer is, of course, oneself. The organizations for which you traded your time for the wherewithal they provided have no memory. They may have said they appreciated you when you supplied a contribution to their cause. But when you're gone, you're gone. You are no longer on the radar screen. It is not a long-term relationship. It works only when it is working.

It is the same for the people you knew. When you were amongst them, you may have had some relevance. But life goes on ... for those whose lives extend beyond yours. This may not have been your intention. But – believe it or not – the real world does not feel obligated to fulfill your intentions, or even to be cognizant of them. Your intentions belong to you. What you do about them depends upon what you do about them, and upon whom you have recruited to aid you as long as you exist. Some cultures revere their forebears. Ours does not. When you are gone, your relevance typically wanes until it becomes extinct. In some cultures, it used to be the convention that your spouse or your lovers would die with you. In our narcissistic culture, people hang around only so long as it pays off for them to do so.

That is not meant to be cynical, or overly negative. It's just the way it is. Even the paper on which this book came to life will most likely disintegrate. We are truth-seekers, not truth-keepers. We believe that what is new is better. About any truth that bears upon our lives, we have little interest. We want to collect "information" about everything. The less it pertains to our lives, the more we want to collect it. The wisdom we collect comes mainly from television commercials, which changes as our culture changes, or as we change. What's most sacred to us is our own opinions. And these change with the people we hang out with. To fade away from other people's mindshare is perhaps the most troubling thing about dying. When you live, you live in other people's minds. When you are no longer a part of *their* lives, you cease to exist. What we forget is that who we were was who we were in other people's minds – a part of their perspective on the world. When we no longer play a role in their lives, we fade away. None of that was what we intended. Things happen in that world outside ourselves that we didn't intend.

The human and natural worlds existed before we arrived. And they will in all likelihood exist after we are gone. We played a very small role in our existence. That small role was what we intended and what we did about our intentions, which may or may not have made us relevant to the larger world beyond ourselves. If we want to leave a legacy, it would have to be how we impacted that larger world with our intentions and what we did about them. We will be remembered only for the consequences of what we did about our intentions.

What Henry David Thoreau wrote in his Journal, 19 July 1851, is pertinent and worth pondering:

> *"Here I am thirty-four years old, and yet my life is almost wholly unexpanded. How much is in the germ! There is such an interval between my ideal and the actual in many instances that I may say I am unborn."*

None of what we know of Thoreau makes us into Thoreau. But it seems to me what he is saying in that our intentions rarely become a part of the "actual" – the real world outside of ourselves. He may be saying that most people arrive and depart having made naught of their intentions. So they might as well have been unborn, given their ideal.

As Nabokov wrote in *Speak, Memory:*

> *"Our existence is but a brief crack of light between two eternities of darkness."*

Intentions are not trivial. We live in a human world made by human intentions having human consequences. What will be the world made for our progeny by *our* intentions?

> *We will be known by the consequences of our intentions.*

5 Intentionality

A term that you could easily spin out of the preceding is *intentionality*. It is as provocative as it is useful. What it means, simply, is that some people live their lives according to their purposes, and some people do not. In a sense, it refers to the condition of having a purpose and being more rather than less addicted to it. Some people are compulsively purposive. Other people may be content to be a part of the flotsam being carried downstream by the pop culture and the happenings of the day. They are content to live their lives by the events of the day. They are event-driven, not purpose-driven.

We will want to know more about this concept of intentionality. It's important, critical to our exploration of intention.

People have intentions, off and on, every day of their early years. As they age, they have fewer. Actually, in cognitive degeneration, they cease to have any but the most immediate. But "having" intentions is quite different from living one's life intentionally. Intentionality refers to a character trait. A person either lives his or her life with intentionality, or does not. People who might be accused of intentionality are intentional about most of their thinking, their feelings, and their actions. Even their conversations with themselves are intentional. A person may have a purpose in mind. But there are those people who function with intentionality – which implies that they have a desired consequence in mind. Merely having a purpose does not clearly emerge from that future outcome implied in intentionality. So it is those who have a future state of affairs in mind who exhibit intentionality. They live more in the way things in the future *should* be – as Don Quixote did. One can have a purpose without wanting to change the present in some *minor* way. People who are intentional want a future outcome that changes the present into that imagined future. Intentionality has more to do with entelechy than with wishful thinking. Entelechy refers to the realization of a potential, to the making of something imagined.

Sculptors especially, as Michelangelo said, in their labors release from the block of marble compelling figures. The potential is there. It just must be realized. It is what artists and composers do. There are a fixed number of black and white keys on a piano keyboard. It is from these that musical compositions have been and still are being made. That is intentionality. In their work, those who are the most intentional change the worlds we inhabit. Out of their intentionality arise different perspectives on the same things. Poets and songwriters have made the concept of love into something as well realized in our minds as Santa Claus. We "know" Santa Claus when we see him.

Many ordinary people can imagine that their lives could be better. But they lack the requisite intentionality to realize those lives in the real world. "Wishing on a star" doesn't do it. Nothing can do it *for them*. They have to do it for themselves. Being able to picture a future and the competence to bring it about is what intentionality can do for people.

That's how important it is.

####

There is a subtle but profound difference between *having* an intention and living one's life *intentionally*. Those who occasionally have an intention are people who live mainly in the past, but are event-driven or routine-driven in the present. Then there are those few people who are driven by their intentions in the present, and this keeps their perspective on the future. The future is where life is. To "fall" in love is to fall for some future state of affairs. That is what is so exciting about it. To remember something of one's past life, even with the evidence of photos or other memorabilia, is not living, but remembering. Or, often those who do not live intentionally try to make a life by living through their children, or through their media regimens. That may fill up one's otherwise lifeless hours. But it is not the same as being *had by* the intentions for one's future. Anticipation, expectation, the life one will have in the future is what turns people on. Looking at someone else's photo collection, or listening to their stories of their past lives turns people off. Over time it turns off the people who like to think that their lives are there, in the past. Where does love go when it leaks out of marriage? It only existed in the future, and now the future is past.

There is an episode in *As Time Goes By* when Jean's ex-sister-in-law comes to visit with her husband after a trip to Spain. She brought packets of photos of their trip. Lionel and Jean exchange hopeless glances at one another. Jean even hides a couple of packets so they don't have to suffer through passing them around. Photos might be meaningful to the people who experienced the images. But other people do not share those same meanings. Their lives are more in their own experiences and not in the images of someone else's experiences. They are dead things, not the same as living things. There is more life in a zip line than there is in other people's past experiences. Vicarious experiences have their uses. But they do not infuse one's own life with expectations as future intentions do.

We anticipate our favorite TV programs or the book we are currently reading. There is no way to anticipate the past. Experiencing life is in the present. But as soon as we are aware of the experience, it has become the past. It's exciting to fall in love, because that can only be consummated in the future. Love doesn't fare well in the present. The present is full of other things. Happiness is at its best in the future or the past. Like love, it is at its best re-experienced either in anticipation or in memory.

In the stories we read about, or the films we attend, there is suspense. The suspense is in the stretch between what is going on in the present and how that twists and turns itself into the future. It's the future we anticipate. How a person became obese doesn't make a particularly appealing story, unless you are becoming obese and maybe don't want to. How a person fell in love is appealing, because most people would like to have that experience. It becomes more appealing as the obstacles that arise between wanting to be there and getting there constitutes the suspense of getting there. Love thrives only where it is wanted, not where it has been had. You can't have the experience of love except by recreating it. The past is past. It is dead. It will not recreate itself, no matter how you try. People who fall out of love experience *that*. But you can't get the experience of falling in love from the experience of falling out of love. Things move in only one direction. And that is the future.

As Gerald Brenan wrote in *Thoughts in a Dry Season*:

> *"Books, places, amusements, people – how*
> *meaningless they become when we suspect*
> *that the person we love loves someone else."*

In a strange sort of way, the person whose life has so little meaning is because that person does not love himself, his life, or his work. Poets are lovers because they arouse the future in us. When a person says her life is meaningless, she is saying that she does not see a future for herself that she can love. It isn't the case that love makes things meaningful. It is only when we can anticipate with pleasure our lives in the future that things (and people, etc.) become so meaningful to us. Painters and sculptors and composers experience this in some measure. Inventors, too. When your life is in the future things are most meaningful to you. Maybe Brenan is saying that it is only when we can anticipate with pleasure our futures that we are really most alive.

Or that any lust for life has to be a lust for one's future? Or that those who lust for the past have already given up on life? Intentionality can only apply to the future. If it is the future one anticipates with expectation, with intention, that is life-giving. All the rest may be just waiting it out.

Thus to live intentionally (intentionality) is to live on that trajectory between now and then. If there is no committed "then," then the present loses its flavor. If there is a "then" to which the individual is committed, then the journey itself is life-giving.

####

If what people say is not what they mean, it becomes difficult if not impossible to guess what they do mean. Saying what one means is a condition of intentionality. For example: People say they want "peace." But peace is not as dramatic as war. So, even though it may not be a conscious intention, people seem to prefer war to peace (whatever that may mean in its particulars). It's a handy slogan, even a cliché to be repeated over and over in different forms. But if war is what turns people on and "peace" that turns people off, they will drift toward war and the threat of war even if it is not a conscious intention but rather a cultural inclination.

Or, to consider a more personal example: People say they want to get married and "live happily ever after." That's the fairy tale. But that isn't what happens. They may even say they will never get married. But the adult world works best with couples, not with singles. So they get married because that is what's done in their culture. After a while, they don't live "happily" but more out of habit and necessity. With that, there is bickering, even shouting matches. Why do half of them get divorced, and the other half go on living lives they never thought they could abide. One young story-book woman says, "How did I get here?"

How, indeed? Often people don't say what they mean because they don't know what they mean by what they say. They do not live intentionally because they have no chosen intentions about what is going on at the moment and thus about their future. If most people have no intentions but immediate ones serving their immediate interests, their destinies must lie elsewhere. In our media and entertainment world, most people get increasingly more of their recipes for living from the media. And the media are notoriously averse to peace, tranquility, and living happily for more than a day or two. They flourish on whatever is not "normal." If peace and happiness were the norm, they would go out of business – especially the "news." Popular novels and videos and movies are made of problems, not recipes for the good life. It is the people and the characters who are *not* normal who get the attention. The most popular "characters" in movies these days are the special events and the suspense. C. Wright Mills offered an intriguing observation in *Power, Politics, and People:*

> *"The mass production of distraction is now as much a part of the American way of life as the mass production of automobiles."*

And that was in 1953. The problem that most people have these days is how to fill their leisure hours with distractions. And those leisure hours have grown and continue to grow. So the distraction industry grows and continues to grow. That is, after all, where the money is. Huge audiences are like a maw, waiting to be fed their daily gruel. So-called wrestling on television would be a good example. But so would the American family waiting for its daily gruel.

And what is a "distraction"? It is something that allows you to live a vicarious life that is far more dramatic and engaging than your own.

> *It appears that living intentionally is the only certain immunity there is for avoiding a life lived by distraction.*

To live (event-driven) in anticipation of one's media fare of distraction seems to becoming the norm. I've seen college students leave their dorms and their acquaintances, walk a few blocks to class with their earphones shutting out the world, and there call or text the people they just departed from. Is their identity so ephemeral that they fear being disconnected from others' devices for even a short period of time? Is it a distraction from what is going on around them that they need and are fearful of losing – of not being in "constant contact"? Those who live by their distractions, it might be said, die by their distractions. Are their distractions efficacious for them, or for those they relate to in some way, or for the society at large?

Intention is not a sometime thing. It is a way of life for those who would choose a way of life. For others, it is trivial, short-lived, of little or no consequence. That one might craft a good life out of one's *worthy* intentions is incomprehensible to them. What is the "fun" in that?

Ideas about "the good life" vary from culture to culture over time and, in our own permissive society, from generation to generation (however that is calculated). In our contemporary world, the younger generation seems to believe that the good life consists of having "fun" and being freed of all responsibility for the consequences of what they think or what they do – or of who they are. They have little use for history, and almost none for any future but their own immediate future. They seem to want to live wholly in the present, caring not that their present quickly becomes their past and the template for their future. They assume that this is their prerogative, and the pop culture supports that assumption.

Still, all of our ways of thinking, of being, and of doing have consequences, not only for them but for the destiny of our collective. There is no way of thinking, there is no practiced perspective, that does not have consequences for any "generation" or for the larger American civilization. Ideas come and go. So do human societies. We make judgments and carry out actions in the name of the ideas currently *de rigueur* for us individuals. The consequences affect us all.

Ideas have consequences for the people who have them. Acted upon, they have consequences not only for those people, but ultimately for all the rest of us.

Intention and Life

The "secrets" of living healthfully are as follows:

- Have no worthy intentions that you can't or don't carry through.

- A "worthy" intention is one that is efficacious – for you, the person who has it, for everyone who has a corroborative stake in your existence, and for any larger collective of which they are a part. That could be a friendship, a marriage, an organization, or the larger society of which you and others are members. As well as the immediate and the abstract "environment."

(This would seem to be a framework for exploration in the next chapter. Here we have some additional angles to be explored.)

- Your biological body will take care of itself – or not. There is little you can do to control its reaction to the circumstances of its life.

- You can medically (or otherwise) ameliorate. Just because it is "yours" doesn't mean that you have total control over it. Things happen. You can control your mind's *interpretation* of what happens in your world. But your body and what happens in your world seem to have logics of their own. You can adapt to the conditions of your life – and even craft your life within the limits imposed by your competencies or those happenings over which you have no control. Some people give up trying to cope with the conditions of their lives.

- By definition, intention has to do with the future. Unless you are seriously impaired by a cognitive disorder, your past is past and you cannot have intentions about your past other than how you might more favorably recollect it. People who have no worthy intentions for their future are generally people who either try to live in the present – or look the other way toward their past. Intentionality channels people to look to the future for their lives, because that's where their lives are going to take place. People who are not channeled by intentionality are sometimes people who pretend to be someone other than who they are. Pretense is easy to detect. It is a condition that is harbored by people who can't, or don't act on, and live by, their worthy intentions. People who live by intentionality are, and are seen as, more authentic. Their pursuit of their intentions is who they *are*. They are forever in the process of becoming who they are as a result of fulfilling their intentions. People who presume that they are determined by their pasts are forever putting on the pretenses that their beliefs about their pasts lead them to. There are thus people who are led by their interpretation of their pasts, and then there are people who are led by their intentions for the future. It has to do with focus. One tries to figure out who they are by explaining the past. The intentional people become who they become as a result of fulfilling their intentions. Over a lifetime, these end up being very different kinds of people in their old age. One succumbs to the diseases of mind and body that come with their past. The other lives on with an eye on what still remains to be done in the future.

- Consider a composer or a playwright. They engage fully in the effort of producing something in their heads that cannot be realized until they can witness it in the real world of the future.
Their intention is to produce something that pleases their audiences sometime in the future. They can fantasize their products, hear them and see them in their mind's-eye. Serious artists toil to perfect a representation of what they imagine. They live their intentionality. Those who do not live this way can only live what they imagine their past requires of them. Or they live a life of pretense, pretending to be whoever others will corroborate. These are two very different ways of living. Some people just intend to be seen as exceptional human

beings, others just as "good" people by the norms extant. Then there are those who want to be seen as remarkable money-makers, or as celebrities. It is one's intentions fulfilled that define people. At the same time, a person may be intolerant or disliked for other reasons, without intending to be.

Intentionality is what helps one to craft his or her own life, which might otherwise be whatever forces play upon them as victims in this world. People are more likely to let the vagaries of whatever occurs in their lives define them. As we have previously considered, the best antidote to being a victim of whatever occurs in your life is to have and pursue worthy intentions.

In her *The Fiery Fountains*, Margaret Anderson wrote:

> *"Once upon a time, many years ago, when I was living happily ever after...."*

That's her ellipsis. What she is intimating, of course, is that life has a way of giving lie to that myth about happiness. We may think we deserve to live "happily ever after." But life in the real world intervenes to cause us to think again. John Osborne, in his *Look Back in Anger*, wrote:

> *"They spend their time mostly looking forward to the past."*

And who is the "they" in his observation? All of the people who do not live life with intentionality – which is most people most of the time. We may wonder what the future "brings." If you do not create the future by claiming it for your own worthy intentions, it will bring whatever it brings, with no concern for your hopes and dreams. Those become the myths you live by. You believe in whatever confirms your intentions. If you have no worthy intentions, the future will confirm that for you, and you will either adapt well to a world you never made, or not.

Their pasts weigh heavily upon those who live there. The more one's past outweighs a person's future, the more compelled they feel to "look forward" to their past. Carl Sandburg addressed this in these lines from his "Prairie":

> *"I tell you that the past is a bucket of ashes.*
> *I tell you yesterday is a wind gone down,*
> *a sun dropped in the west.*
> *I tell you there is nothing in the world*
> *only an ocean of tomorrows*
> *a sky of tomorrows."*

So the choice that people make about not having any intentions in life that they *have to* fulfill is that of having only an arrested life. Sandburg is saying that there is nothing in the world but an ocean of tomorrows. If that's the only thing in the world, then one ought to live there – intentionally. If needed, one might consider the anonymous saying: *"The past is a prison for those who live in it."*

Indeed it is. Our pasts become weightier the longer we live. So it sort of seems like human nature to live there. How does it become a "prison"? It keeps those who live there from living in the ocean of tomorrows. And the only ticket there is to get out of there is to decide what your

worthy intentions are for your life, and then to do what
has to be done to realize them.

####

Intentionality has to do with what we give our attention
to in our everyday lives. As difficult as it may seem, there
is a simple way of measuring this. It's a take-off of that
much tossed-about economic expression, ROI – which is
intended to refer to the returns you get for how you invest
your money. In this case, it is your ROA – your return on
what you give your attention to, or how you invest your
mind.

It is your mind that circumscribes what you will pay
attention to. We see and hear what we expect to see and
hear. That varies from person to person and subculture
to subculture. Plumbers have a lower threshold about
plumbing subjects. Physicians see and hear other
physicians differently then they do patients. Cosmologists
have a lower threshold for images or talk about cosmology
than do miners. Young lovers may devote far more time
talking to one another than they devote to their learning.
It is our minds that provide us with the meaning of
things that happen inside or outside of us. And it is the
immediate *meaning* of things that captures our attention.
We may think that we control our attention. Most of the
time, this is not so. We invest our attention in what is
most meaningful to us at the moment. And that is a
habitual thing most of the time, not an intentional thing.
To be intentional about how you invest your attention
in things requires you *not* to pay attention to anything
that is irrelevant to your intentions and to pay attention
to things happening in your sensory environment that
might bear upon your intentions. People who have no

long-range intention end up paying attention to whatever is going on at the moment. That takes those people where those happenings go, not where they might want to go. They are victims not of their intentions, but victims of whatever piques their attention at the moment. They don't do triage on what is going on. People who are serving their intentions do.

That makes a big difference in what you become in life. It has often been observed (by better observers than most people seem to be) that we become what we pay attention to. Ortega Y Gasset described it thus:

> *"Tell me to what you pay attention and I will tell you who you are."*

People are always in the process of becoming who they are. And this is done cumulatively by how they invest their attention. Infants "imprint" on their parents and siblings and care-givers because that's all they have available. What's available expands exponentially as they grow. But some people never choose wisely (because they are not wise). Most people don't think it is important, they don't think it is critical to what they become. But it is. The more mind share people give to something over time, the more it will influence who they become, as unaware as they may be of that influence. People who deal with numbers every hour of every day are likely to become digits in the scheme of things. People who dote on their pets are likely even to look like their pets over time.

If what people pay attention to is worthy – even ideal – they are likely to become worthier themselves – even ideal. Marcus Aurelius put it in these terms:

> *"Every [person] is worth just so much as*
> *the worth of what [they] have set their heart*
> *upon."*

Idealistic, of course. He was after all a spokesman for the Roman ideal. If you substitute intentions for the word "heart," you have a very pragmatic view of the path the be taken, reminiscent of the more ancient *Tao-te-Ching* (the Chinese book of "the way" to live a good life). If you do not aim for the ideal, you will be aiming for something less, the path apparently taken by more and more people.

The "input" side is that of what we pay attention to in our lives, and what kind of returns we get on that investment. For people who are concerned about their ROA, they will also be concerned about what kind of consequences there will be as a result of who they are – of who they have become. The more human the ideal they achieve, the better for all of those with whom they have contact. An ideal friend influences one to become an ideal friend. In the same way, a less than ideal friend influences others to be less than ideal.

We do not live in a culture that establishes criteria for what constitutes the ideal. Nor does our culture encourage that. It is almost as if "freedom" is license to practice less than the ideal. So if a person is to pursue the ideal in our culture, they must do so against the grain. They must be contrarians. This may have always been the case, as Sun Tzu through Machiavelli must have assumed. The more contemporary Japanese novelist Soseki Natsume thought of the dilemma in this way:

> *"Freedom without great ideals is nothing but*
> *decadence."*

In other words, our modern idea of "freedom" may actually be that of freedom *from* those great ideals. It may be no more than freedom from responsibility for the consequences of one's thoughts and actions – quite the opposite of living by great ideals. And what is "decadence"? A turn toward extinction? One must intend to pursue the ideal. One can justify his or her existence in a million other ways. No one ever had the intention of being wrong.

Norman Douglas said *"You can tell the ideals of a nation by its advertisements."* That's where most people get their more immediate intentions as consumers who converse with other consumers. Are there any ideals concerned in being a consumer of whatever is in fashion? Thomas Carlyle said:

> *"I do not believe in the collective wisdom of individual ignorance."*

Could this be taken to mean that democracy erodes all ideals? How can a society be put on the right track for its destiny by people who have no worthy (ideal) intentions? Does ignorance have any measure other than the ideal? It has been said that people know what they want by knowing what others want. What is it we want? What is the ideal being served by being in step with others? Carlyle does indeed raise some interesting questions about *intentionality*. Can mediocrity ever be anyone's worthy intention? Can the worthiness of any intention be measured in any way but its consequences first for that person, and then for all the rest of us?

H. G. Wells, who was more intelligent than you may have assumed, offered us this valuable perspective on success in life. If you were going to live intentionally, can you think of a more inclusive criterion than this one?

> *"Wealth, notoriety, place and power are no measure of success whatever. The only true measure of success is the ratio between what we might have done and what we might have been on the one hand, and the thing we have made of ourselves on the other."*

In other words, did you make of the raw material all that could possibly have been made of it? Intentionality makes *bricoleurs* of those who live their lives that way. A bricoleur is a person who accomplishes what needs accomplishing with the tools and resources at hand. As he or she acquires more conceptual tools and resources, they can accomplish more. They grow by adding to their repertoire. They are inherently learners, not stunted by what they happen to know.

Living intentionally is a matter of living by questions. Why is this the best way to live – by being curious about anything that might bear upon your intentions? Are you on the right path? How could you know (or why would you even wonder) if you were not living intentionally?

It is intention that gives the richest meanings to life. Those who have lost their way (if they ever had one) have despaired of their intentions in life. Colors fade. They go through life as if they were robots, except as they are anxious that robots are going to displace them.

Any worthy life is buoyed by intention. That's intentionality.

6 Lying, Duplicity, & Deceit

People lie to themselves...routinely. People lie to other people...frequently. They might not do so if the pop culture didn't encourage it. But they might. There has never been a culture where appearances didn't matter. The clothes we wear are intended to "communicate" to others who we are. If you wear loafers without socks, you are pretending to be an executive. You may wear eye make-up, or a bra that exaggerates, intending to be seen as more glamorous than you may be when you wake up in the morning. We want to look fashionable, and yet distinguish our status in the world by how much we can spend to get the "look" that we and others wear and do to identify us by. Our clothes and coiffures are often not who we are, but who we intend to be in public.

We cover our bodies with signs of status – essentially what we can buy to tell others who we are. How much we can pay for shoes matters. So does the car we buy. So does our home or apartment décor. So do the watches we wear or the pens we use. We are actors on our stage – be it large or small. How we comport ourselves when with others is intended to "communicate" to them our superiority or inferiority. We practice being seen. We pose just so in order to seduce them into seeing us as we would like to be seen. For the Maori of New Zealand, their social status could be determined by those who were capable of "reading" their body markings. Not much has changed. We whiten our teeth. We do so in order to appear superior to those whose teeth are not as white, whose skin is not as "clear," or whose buying power is not as great.

There is who we "are" (whatever that means). And then there is how we would like other people to see us. We accessorize our minds, our bodies, and our cars, homes, clothing and comportment. We do this primarily to be seen as we would like to be seen. We do not always succeed. It's tough to appear intelligent in a group of intelligent people. It's not so hard to be seen as successful in a group of people who aren't. But of course, the people in either group can be fooled by a competent deceiver some of the time (as Lincoln said).

If you can deceive yourself, you will be able to deceive others. Emerson wrote in his Journal in 1852:

> *"A [person] cannot dupe others long, who has not duped oneself first."*

Emerson may have this circularity wrong. Young children learn to dupe others first, and this makes duping themselves possible. They grow up in a culture that condones deceit. So they learn how they may have been deceived, and how to deceive others for their benefit. People vary greatly in their capacity for being duped, and for duping themselves. Skeptics, for example, like physicians, are more readily duped by what appears to be "scientific" than what appears to be no more than the news of the day. Religious folk are more likely to be duped by religious-sounding material than by agnostic tracts. Entertainers are more likely to be duped by their fans than their critics. Lovers are more susceptible to being duped by their lovers than by their parents. And so on.

The point is that all people are capable of being duped, and of duping others. Those who think they are impervious to being duped are easy targets for those who can readily read their susceptibilities. We are not on-guard for anything for which we have a low threshold. We have a high threshold for anything that might not confirm who we are or how we think or believe. We are not open to anything that conflicts with what we already know. We are quite open to anything we might see or hear that confirms who we are, what we believe, or is otherwise complimentary. We are open to the world as long as that world supports us and the way our minds work. If and when it doesn't, we get angry and put on our armor. Or we attack it. A mass murderer is a person who hates the world he lives in and tries to destroy it in any way that seems in fashion. A mass murderer becomes a media celebrity. A law-abiding citizen doesn't. That's the world we live in. If a person is going to shoot you, it probably won't change anything to ask him or her not to do so. Would it for you if you had already armed yourself to punish the world for not caring about you the way you thought would be providential? If you get in the way of a very angry person, that person may just run you over.

You may have intentions about the way the world should be – to be satisfactory to you – but there is always someone else in the word who thinks it should be their way. You cannot pursue your intention in a vacuum, because there isn't one. For every action you intend to take, there will be a reaction. That reaction is not likely to be consistent with your action. You may think your intentions should be catered to by your world or your social circle, but your world does not care. And your social circle is busy with their own intentions, not yours.

####

You can harbor what you think to be the best intentions in the world.

But the world does not care about your intentions. You may think that you *deserve* more complicity with respect to your intentions on the part f your world. But your world does not exist to be complicit with your (or anyone else's) intentions. It is the way it is because it got to be that way. Your world is indifferent to your intentions. Your world does not exist to be beneficent to your intentions. It is neither objective nor subjective. It is indifferent. You will be duped. If you live in a world where you can be or cannot be duped, that's the world you live in. You can't buy a gun or a bomb that can kill your culture. But you can buy a gun or a bomb that can kill you. Don't waste your time on things you can't do anything about. If you try to fix yourself or your world by "wishing on a star," go ahead and try it. It doesn't work.

So here's the picture: You live in a world that has a few billion people in it. You have intention after intention all day every day. So does everyone else. Your intentions may be somewhat compatible with those who share your subcultures. But your intentions are likely to be in conflict with (or irrelevant to) those of at least several billion other people. That's why it's never easy to carry out your own intentions. The other reason is simply that you may not be competent enough to do so – given the real world beyond your private intentions.

To have your way in the world, you will probably have to con other people. But they are busy conning you. So where does this get you? You may have to connive to be who you want to be, or to do what you want to do. No use complaining. No one else cares what your intentions are...unless those intentions conflict with theirs. Then they may have to thwart your intentions, or you may have to thwart their intentions. So what the infant or the adult has to learn is that there are other people in their world. And those other people have intentions of their own. They will either be indifferent or contentious. Collectively, they can run you over. Individually, they may best you with a more appealing intention or by being more competent or influential at making things go their way.

Which may serve to bring us here...

In *Doctor Zhivago*, Boris Pasternak wrote:

> *"The great majority of us are required to live a life of constant, systematic duplicity. Your health is bound to be affected if, day after day, you say the opposite of what you feel, if you grovel before what you dislike and rejoice at what brings you nothing but misfortune."*

He is of course writing about how to live a healthier life. But our culture *requires* us to live a life of duplicity: of not saying what we believe, but saying or doing something that fits the circumstances and the people involved. We are like puppets, habituated to the condition of saying what we think other people want to hear. We play games with others – saying what we think will bring about the consequences we want for ourselves. We lie in order to be seen by others as smarter or more desirable than we really are. That life of duplicity takes its toll on one's health, as Dr. Zhivago said. Candidates for a job at your organization tell lies to be thought as better than they really are. Candidates for a love affair tell lies in order to seduce the other. We hide ourselves in order to have a public persona that we imagine will get us where we want to go. Politicians do this all the time. We are all politicians.

Even though he had much good advice for his Prince, Machiavelli is often denounced for advising his Prince that furthering the interests of the state for which he was responsible might require him to be duplicitous. If you have to deal with people who are duplicitous, you may have to be duplicitous. In other words, if another person is trying to deceive you, you may have to try to deceive the other person. In a world becoming a modern world, you may be *required* to be duplicitous, to say something that isn't true. As a good, pragmatic philosopher, this is what Machiavelli wrote to one of his many overlords, as recorded in "The Truth About Machiavelli" by Murray Kempton in *New Republic* (11 March 1967):

> *"For a long time I have not said what I believed nor do I ever believe what I say, and if indeed sometimes I do happen to tell the truth, I hide it among so many lies that it is hard to find."*

Few people would be that candid. Why hide the truth? After a lifetime of duplicity, it is hidden even from the person talking. He or she has become so habituated to deceiving others that if they do happen to tell the truth, it would no longer be discernable as the truth. The truth is hidden from them because they very rarely look at themselves without seeing instead their persona. Do men in high places tell the truth? Their competencies lie elsewhere. That's what Machiavelli is trying to tell us in his confession. Is he telling the truth? We can't know, can we? And isn't that in part because duplicity has become normative? We learn how to deceive. In doing so, we end up deceiving ourselves. The better we are at deceiving others, the better we become at deceiving ourselves.

In a world where duplicity is required, we no longer know (or perhaps care) what the truth might be. We don't need it to get along. In the modern world we all inhabit, telling the truth would strike most people as a con. Telling the truth is not *de rigueur*. Duplicity is.

Boxing, a long-time popular sport, is based on duplicity – feigning one thing but doing another. To a certain extent, so are chess and poker. And so is life in our world.

It may not be intentional on your part to deceive others. No matter. Where it is normative – required – you will do so. What is normative is like our air is to us. We breathe it in and out without actually being aware of it. It is obvious that even young children can say "I love you," without being concerned about the truth of it. If it works, it works. In *The Passionate State of Mind*, Eric Hoffer wrote:

> *"Self-deception, credulity, and charlatanism are somehow linked together."*

What he is suggesting to those who have any curiosity about such things is that to the extent we deceive ourselves, we are culpable in being readily deceived by others, and capable of being charlatans where others are concerned. Did we ever actually intend this? No, it is one of those things that we imbibe from our culture with no intention to do so, like speaking English. It is probably easy to conclude that no infant chooses his or her native tongue. Once again, we lie and deceive others because it is the norm in our culture. Our duplicity is expected. We couldn't get by in our culture by telling the truth – for example, that the person you are talking to is ugly, or stupid. It may be true. But we don't say that to the person's face. We save it for our gossip about that person when in the company of others who think the same thing, but do not say so.

In *Glimpses of World History,* Nehru himself wrote:

> *"It is amazing how people deceive themselves and others when it is to their interest to do so."*

Toddlers learn this early. Adults acknowledge this sooner or later. But it is not anything new. It was perhaps as common to early, literate people as it is to us moderns. Isn't it commonplace that people deceive themselves when looking at a "selfie" or a mirror? If there is something to be gained by deceiving others, who would fail to do so? Your lover? Your favorite philosopher? Does your physician see you as you see yourself? If you feel compassion for a dying friend, isn't that feeling ultimately a selfish one? Isn't it your intention to make yourself feel better by expressing concern? You are doing what is normative – what is called-for in such circumstances. Can you take credit for your intentions in that situation? Why is it that we save our positive feelings for one another for birthdays, or Valentine's Day, or even Christmas? Isn't it the treatment we receive from those others on the other 364 days a year that matter more? Is there ever a time when we are dealing with others that we do so with no concern whatsoever for our own interests?

So our intentions are often not our own intentions at all, but merely our sense of the protocol required. And when we do undertake an intention consciously, it is always colored by our own interests. So there is little altruism in our intentions. Do others know this? Or are they of personal necessity just being credulous? And when is it to anyone's self-interest not to be credulous?

Are we lying when we say "I love you"? Are we lying when we take an oath that we will be true, and that we will care for this other person in perpetuity, whatever the circumstances? Apparently, most people are, since so very few live happily ever after. They bicker, they often cease to care, they drift apart, they begin to see the other person from a more selfish perspective. Maybe they meant what they said on the day they got married or began to co-habit. But people change. "Always" becomes too much of a prison. They are never the person the other person fell in love with. So let's say they were not lying when they were falling in love. Later on, they would be lying if they uttered those words. But they often do, out of habit, or hoping to change the other. It may be that their duplicity is not intended. If it is not intended, are they lying? Or is the lie in the consequences for one or both?

Some people act on their intentions. Most people seem not to have any intentions of their own. They just act according to the news or the commercials or the happenings of the day. There are always those people who think of themselves as the center of the universe. They seem incapable of de-centering themselves, of seeing anything other than the way *they* see the world. Young people today seem to believe that the world began the day they were born. Older people like to be perplexed by what has become of the world they once knew, or once dreamed of. We are consumers like pigs at the trough. We consume more entertainment in a week than our forebears could ever have imagined in their lifetimes.

We are outwardly opinionated, whether we know anything about the subject being discussed or not. People who have no real beliefs march with others for some belief or other. They expend more energy on some cause or other than they ever did on their own lives. The less people know about what is actually going on, the more passionately (or for pay) they take up their causes.

The relationship – if any – between intention and dedicated actions seems to be a conundrum, or a nest of conundrums. While the two may have been inseparable in prior times, or in other cultures, they seem in our culture to be treated as two independent things. Why do people do what they do? We don't any longer know, or care. We simply want the objective or "scientific" answer. And the intentions of science seem to play less and less a role. So people sometimes commit suicide. What was it about their background or their environment that *caused* them to do that? Surely they did not *choose* to do what they did. When mind was thrown out of the formula because it is not tangible, material, and reducible, we ended up with seemingly insoluble conundrums. The scientizers would like us to live in a cause-and-effect world, totally rational and reducible to some explanation that even they would understand. The world is full of people. And those people think about things, and sometimes they have intentions that only *they* presume to understand.

If all that we think or believe or do is simply caused by forces beyond our control, what hope is there for humankind? And if this is problematical, what are we to do with those experts who explain our predicament – since their explanations are necessarily also caused by forces over which *they* have no control? Are the Explainers (the scientizers) telling us lies? How could they? They are as *caused* as they assume the rest of us are. Some examples may provoke us to think a little bit more insightfully about some of the conundrums we have brought upon ourselves by throwing the baby (the mind) out with the bathwater (the consequences of our own follies):

- If a politician promises you whatever you want for your vote, who is lying to whom?

- If you can't help believing any person who says "I love you," who is lying to whom?

- If you believe those who agree with you but refuse to believe those who don't agree with you, which one of you is lying?

- If your mother told you a lie, would you believe her?

- If someone said, "Don't worry, I will take care of you," under what conditions would you believe that person?

- If someone you didn't know called to tell you that you had won a prize, when would you start asking, "What's the catch?"

- If identifying a scammer requires you to know what their tricks of the trade are, where would you get that intelligence and why would you believe it?

- If you had never told a lie, how would you know what a lie is?

- If a used-car salesman told you how great you look sitting at the wheel of the car you are drawn to, what would your first thought be? What would your next question be?

- In a boxing match, or a high-stakes poker game, you know that the other(s) are out to deceive you. Can you win by telling them the truth? Or must you out-deceive them?

- In a competitive basketball game, your advantage lies in faking-out the one whose role it is to keep you from scoring. Is it any different in our world?

- Machiavelli advised his Prince that there were people out there who would take advantage of him if he weren't capable of taking advantage of *them*? Seems like life in the real world?

- Why is it always only the "bully" who is to blame?

- Would the service tech you called cheat you – if he thought he could get away with it?

- Ever known anyone who cheated on their taxes?

- Why is it so commonplace for people to lie under oath – as in a courtroom or on television? What was it Bill Clinton said at first?

- If things work the way they do because "everybody" is doing it, who is telling a lie?

- If you had your choice of telling the truth, or of telling a lie that would be far more beneficial to you, what would you do?

- If you had the intention of starting a diet regime tomorrow, but did not do so, who is lying to whom?

- If your President said, "It is our intention to put a man on the moon in this decade," but that didn't happen, was he lying? To whom, about what?

- When is a promise not a promise?

- When two nations fight a war, each intends to win the war. So what does the loser say about losing?

- Were those who were burned at the stake for being "witches" telling the truth? Were their accusers telling the truth? What possible difference would that make for the one who was burned to death?

- Let's say you crashed someone else's car and killed a person. Is that person any less dead if that wasn't your intention?

- You said you would love that person until death do you part. You didn't. Was the lie in the original covenant, or in your later transgression?

- People who have beautiful bodies or faces due to genetics beyond their control often appear as models hawking some product in the media. If it is a product they in fact don't use, are they lying? Are they doing so for money? Anyone you know who wouldn't?

- Your celebrities often appear in the media endorsing some product or service. If they don't actually use that product or service, are they lying – for money or more publicity?

- One spouse in a marriage decides to make the marriage better. But, as is said, "It takes two to tango." If the other spouse doesn't collaborate, what happens to the intention?

- Social movements begin with some person's or small group's intentions. If they become faddish or fashionable, they are likely to become embedded in the culture. If some people don't concur, but are affected by them anyway, what would you call that – influence without representation? How universal is that?

- In organizations of all kinds and sizes, the chief executive may have some good intentions. But the more people involved in implementing those good intentions, the less likely they are to turn out as intended.

- Of the billions of people who have intentions that can impact you every day, which ones are you going to endorse and implement?

- People are out to scam you every day, given the level of your gullibility. The best ones work in the media. They're the professionals. The rest – your friends and acquaintances – are the amateurs. How do ordinary people gain immunity, if indeed they intend to have any?

- Would your grocer deceive you for his or her own benefit? Would your pastor?

- How did you get so effective at deceiving yourself?

In his Journal (of 6 December 1813), Lord Byron wrote:

> *"One lies more to one's self than to anyone else."*

That can't be just because we talk more to ourselves than we talk to anyone else. What part does the pop culture play in this self-deceit? And (again) if it is the norm, what is to be done about it? There comes a time when everyone gets so good at it that they no longer realize they are lying to themselves. Is this their intention? A toddler doesn't care whether what they do or say is lying or not. This seems to be even more characteristic of most adults. *Where lying and deception are the norm, to speak the truth would earn you the epithet of being a liar.*

If you like paradoxes in your life, that may be the first one. In a cannibalistic culture, the person who refuses the gift may be beaten or even killed. Witches still exist. And if you think you are above your culture, you may quickly learn you are not. Your culture will carry you downstream or upstream. But it is not there to serve your personal worthy (or unworthy) intentions.

There is a price to be paid to harbor or implement even the best of intentions. (Try to do so in any bureaucracy and you will see. The folk wisdom is: *In any bureaucracy, no good deed will ever go unpunished.*)

That bureaucracy may be a well-intended marriage gone astray, to an organization having thousands of employees – for example, a government bureaucracy.

If you are unwilling or incapable of paying the price to do so, then there is very little reason for you to harbor or to try to implement any worthy intention.

Living by your intentions (i.e., with a worthy purpose in mind) is the best way to live, even if all you can do is optimize the consequences of your intentions. The outcome is never likely to be perfect, but the pursuit is life-giving. To live in any way but intentional is to have no more than a truncated life. Giving up on your worthy intentions is a form of suicide...of your spirit. It is true, that no one is going to get out of this life alive. But it is what you make of it that matters. Recall the words of H.G. Wells:

> *"Wealth, notoriety, place and power are no measure of success whatever. The only true measure of success is the ratio between what we might have done and what we might have been on the one hand, and the thing we have made of ourselves on the other."*

That ratio is the one created by the pursuit of worthy intentions.

But if you intend to pursue your intentions in the real world, it helps (immensely) to have the right perspective. The world is not as complicit as it may seem in the movies, or television, or in the commercial media.
After all, those predators make their money off of you by deceiving you – making you think they are doing you a

favor. They are not. They are doing themselves a favor. So what Wells is saying may be just a matter of doing what he says. That's never as easy as it may seem – which is why it is easy to agree, but extremely difficult to carry out. He is saying that success in life has only one true measure: *the ratio between what you made of your life and what you **could have** made of your life.* The real world doesn't exist to enable you personally to make a success of your life. To the contrary. It seems more likely to exist to provide you with obstacles to making a success of your life. And it does seem to depend upon how worthy your intentions were, and how capable you were of implementing them in the environment within which you had to do so.

One could readily accept the proposition that being incarcerated in the Nazi death camps left its occupants little choice. When you are struggling just to survive, or even if you have everything you need, you may not be imagining that there is an option to make of your life a better life.

7 Promises, Promises

A liar is a person who says one thing but behaves in ways inconsistent with what he or she says. In other words, he or she is trying to deceive you by promising one thing but delivering another. If you tell someone (yourself, even) that you are reading this, but you are not really reading this, you have made a statement tantamount to a promise (as all such statements are). Why there is no *necessary* correlation between what people say and what people do is a fundament of all communication. We may expect people to be as good as their word, but most aren't. We make the most, it would seem, of our pop culture notion of "free speech" – which may mean to most people that they and everyone else can say whatever they want about whatever they want whenever they want. It is up to those on the receiving end to sort out what it means, if anything. Our pop culture says we can do this without compunction. In other words, someone can accuse you in public of wrongdoing without a shred of evidence.

At one time in our evolution, people may have felt an obligation to tell the truth (as they saw it). Certain words and certain actions were taboo. In our legalistic (vs. moral) society, the issue is whether or not you have broken some law. You haven't. The one you have maligned is the one purported to have broken some law. You can accuse at will. It is up to the accused to seek legal recourse for any damage to her life or her reputation. With no substantial evidence whatsoever, a person can accuse you of sexual harassment. It is up to you to prove your innocence, if that is what's at stake. You are guilty until proven innocent – which certainly turns moral turpitude (if not a basic right in the Bill of Rights section of the Constitution) on its head. But ours is a legalistic society, not a moralistic society.

It is illegal to lie under oath. But people do it all the time. They are only "guilty" if someone else intends to go to the trouble (and the cost) to challenge them. In other words, people make promises but do not always keep them. They may think they're just "words." But words are what the mind is made of, and minds are what all relationships and societies are made of. Everything is made of words. Communication is the infrastructure of *everything* human – including human relationships and human societies. The more abused words are, the more abusive the relationship or the society will be.

A statement is a premise. So every statement – like "I love you" – is a kind of promise. It promises that what is implied can be depended upon. If the statement is a physics theorem, it promises that it will hold up under scrutiny. In mathematics, $2 + 2 = 4$. What can't be proved is a lie, an attempt to deceive. Words don't carry the same dependability. It's the consequences we're after. Whether "I love you" works for the speaker is what's at stake, not the validity of the words deployed. For example, what does the word "I" mean? Since the "I" of 15 years hence is not the "I" of today, is it even *possible* to lie? What does the word "love" mean, empirically? It seems to mean different things to different people. If that is the case, then when the parent wielding the switch with the statement, "I'm doing this for your own good," it must be because that parent loves his or her child. Who is to say that parent isn't doing so for the child's own good? Or is the parent doing it because it makes the parent feel better?

Promises are tricky things in our culture. You may promise to pay your credit card bill when due. But some people don't keep their promises. So the penalty is stiff. Then there is another question: Did the credit card company tell *you* what the penalty was? No, they just offered you a printed form that carried a statement about what happened to people in general if they didn't pay their bill on time. Is that the same as telling *you* personally? So did they try to deceive you for their own benefit? After all, at 25% interest, they may be hoping that you *don't* pay your bill on time. It may pass the legal test. But would it pass the moral test?

So who is the "you" in that everyday assertion "I love *you*"? People fall in love with the mental image they have of the other person. Is that the same thing as that other person? If they are delusional, are they culpable? If they follow the fashion and decide to get married, and if after being married for a while, decide it is not what they thought, is the promise they made in public really enforceable? Should it be? If your grocer sells you something that is rotten, can you take it back and get your money back? In some cases, yes. So what exactly is the difference between the two? The grocer offered. You paid. You don't think you got what you paid for. So you want to give it back and get your money back.

What *is* the *implied* warranty in a marriage? That you get what you paid for in time and effort as well as in dollars? Sometimes the vagaries of life in our society make liars of all of us. We know that citizenship requires us all to pay taxes according to the provision of the tax laws at the time. Do we ever "fib" a little in order to lower our taxes? Do rich people? They can afford the roomful of accountants and lawyers looking for loopholes.

Can you? Should the IRS be required to point out those loopholes to everyone just to be "fair"? If the laws favor the rich, who made the laws?

In the real world, things get far more convoluted than this. So exactly what is it that we lower class people were promised? If you don't like the deal you got (comparatively), can you take your return back and get your money back?

####

Louis Howe, who was Presidential Assistant to FDR, said in a speech at Columbia University (17th January 1933):

> *"You can't adopt politics as a profession and remain honest."*

This is applicable, as we all know, because it is equally true that you can't adopt the modern society as a performer in it and remain honest. The pop culture essentially requires it of you. The higher your status, the more it requires that of you. Your doctor, for example, will probably neglect to inform you that the new drug he or she is writing you a script for comes with a (much-needed?) kickback. Nor would your lawyer inform you that much legal work is predatory: they have arranged to make themselves available when you increasingly need some legal help. Even your pastor might suggest that making a sizable contribution to the church could well enhance your chances of going to heaven. Your insurance agent may neglect to inform you that at one time the four or five most profitable firms in the country were insurance companies. They get rich off of their actuarial schemes. You may buy a ticket to watch your favorite team play. But it comes with no guarantee that your fanship will contribute to the other team losing. The "best" soda on the market is not the one that is the best for your health. The "best" toothpaste is simply the one you are most likely to buy because it is the "best." Commercial advertising offers you the best of everything – anything and everything that has the promise of making money for the advertisers and their clients. Whatever makes you a "better" consumer is the ultimate product of marketing. But you knew that, correct?

Most of us would like a better life. That's our susceptibility and it is at the same time every marketer's dream. It would be miraculous if there were anyone in business, including your landscaper, who is in it for *your* benefit. They promise. You pay. It's the world we live in.

It's a difficult word: *promise.* It is paradoxical. It raises people's hopes at the same time it is setting them up for letting them down, as Cyril Connolly intimated. A person may promise eternal love. But most don't know what they mean by that. It may be his or her intention. But one's intention may turn out to be short-lived. And the person who is being addressed doesn't really know what that means. What it really means can only be known in some distant future. The problem with intention is that it has to be realized – to be created, to be brought about in the real world. It is the same for promise. It can only be seen for what it is at some point in the future. Intention, like promise, is best know for its shelf life. So an intention is like a promise to oneself. We can't know if it exists until it bears some fruit. If it doesn't, it dies on the vine. It is the same with promises made to others. Their worth lies in whether or not they were fulfilled.

To live well, a person needs to have intentions. That's the promise. Whether or not that promise is fulfilled is the only way of knowing how valid it is. By not fulfilling one's intentions, one invalidates oneself. By not fulfilling one's promises, one invalidates oneself...socially. Your reputation – how you are known by others – depends on how often your promises to them are empty. You shall know them by their fruits, our Bible says. A person whose worthy intentions do not bear fruit becomes barren. As Connolly described it, *"promise is the capacity for letting people down."* The person who is most affected by being let down is the person who makes the promise. Maybe your spouse doesn't care what you promised, because he or she no longer cares one way or the other. But a worthy intention that does not bear fruit makes a private mockery of the person who harbors it. Thus the saying: *Don't promise what you cannot deliver.*

How is a person to know that? An infant's intention to walk is undeterred by falls and obstacles. It will be accomplished, with only minor exceptions. Where did we lose that perspective? Why is it that some people still have it and some people don't? Does it have anything to do with the guilt felt at not keeping one's promises to oneself?

If you intend to be a good reader, what would you have to do? If you want your love to grow, what would you have to do? If you want your capabilities to grow in the roles you have chosen, or have fallen into, what would you have to do? Epictetus, as you may know, was a Greek slave. He studied and observed. When he became a free man, he also became a noted philosopher. He put the answer to "the good life" to us as starkly as has ever been done.

We make the art of living seem far too complicated, and too daunting. What Epictetus advised was simply this:

"First, say to yourself what you would be; then do what you have to do."

Epictetus was a frugal thinker – a lesson no one in the hierarchy of the public education bureaucracy seems to have gotten. But we can make much of his frugal advice, and have. We have brushed by this before. But it bears revisiting.

First, most people seem not to have any concrete intention about what they could be, or should be. Second, most people do not seem to make that promise, which Epictetus describes simply as "say to yourself what you would be." Some people complain about their lot in life, even though most never were slaves. In your most unleashed imagination, what would you *be* in this world? Maybe that is just too paradoxical. The more choices you have, the less likely it is that you will make any certain, committed choice. The British (and of course other) royals have the choice already made for them. To be the Queen, perform at all times in public as the Queen. So, carrying out what he refers to as the first step is beyond most people. Some people seem to know by age five. Others never seem to know. But it is the *sine qua non.* If you can't take that first step, the rest of it is irrelevant.

If you do have a plausible image of what you "would be," then there is the next challenge, which is, as Epictetus so blithely put it: *then do what you have to do.* That is far easier said than done, as he would have known. He doesn't presume to tell you what that is, because he had no way of knowing what you would be, or whether you had the right capabilities for doing it. Those capabilities are roughly two:

- You are capable of seeing clearly what it is you would have to do, and to see what the path is like in your environment given your competencies.

- You need to know what the obstacles are – within yourself and in that environment – and whether or not you can be faithful to your intention (your promise to yourself) and thus persevere. He didn't say all you would need was the desire. What you would have to do requires not just the ability to see it, but the wherewithal to do it, such as determination. If it were easy, you would already have done it.

Most people seem not to have what it takes to mount that kind of distant perspective. They would rather take it day at a time, whatever comes along. But if Epictetus could rise from slavery to philosophize as he did, it is doable. It reminds one of how Viktor Frankl wrote about what he learned from surviving the holocaust. Some people do have intentions and live to demonstrate them. Horowitz was considered at the time to be the best concert pianist in the 20th-century. He was asked on the day he died, "What did you do yesterday?" His reply was, "I practiced." That's following through on one's intention.

There was also the interesting film, *It's a Beautiful Life*, about a father's concern for his son in the death camps. The father interpreted their lives there as fiction – which is what most lives are – so that the impact on his son was far better than it might otherwise have been. No one can constrain your interpretation of your condition, no matter how bad others think that is. Ursula Le Guin and Penelope Lively (in her book *Making It Up)* both wrote about this, albeit from quite different perspectives. There have always been observers of the human condition who suggested that what we can imagine is real, and that what we take to be reality (our mass delusion) is the fiction. Einstein suspected. Szasz provided the argument.

So to follow Epictetus's advice may be the healthiest way to live – when your intentions are more real to you than what people take to be "reality." Don Quixote (a fictional character who has outlived several generations of his readers) saw the world as he believed it ought to be rather than as it was generally taken to be. He is often portrayed as a buffoon. But he didn't just *have* intentions. He lived them. We can imagine the remarkable differences between merely having intentions and living them. Is Quixote's continued appeal that he was onto something the rest of us should seriously consider? After all, *we* may be the "buffoons."

This has probably occurred to you...that breaking a promise you had made brought with it more dramatic excitement than you would have experienced by keeping that promise. Exemplifying certain norms of your subculture may have its rewards. But so does giving lie to your promises. The reward for breaking your promises is that it is more of a turn-on for you if you fail to do what others expect you to do. That's the appeal of being dishonest but getting away with it. You've probably had that feeling. The risk is that you may not get away with it. The suspense involved in it is what makes it exciting.

Lies are like that. If you get away with it, a lie brings its own reward: exhilaration. There is not much exhilaration in telling the truth. Telling a lie and getting away with it is exhilarating – ask any professional politician or courtroom lawyer...or the Marquis de Sade. Seducing people by telling them lies has its own perverse reward. Following the "rules" can be boring, as many married people will admit. But even fantasizing an extramarital affair can be exciting. A person who lives solely by the rules of the game is often dull, boring. It is the person who breaks the rules, like our favorite celebrity, who appeals to us. Have you read any good books lately? What makes them "good"?

What it comes down to is that a person who doesn't keep his or her promises is more interesting to us than someone who does. This may be no more than a perversity of our peculiar culture. But it may also serve to justify trying to be more interesting to oneself. We like to think that our time is more "modern," and therefore different, even superior (our thinking tainted by the notion of "evolution"). But here is the Fifth-century B.C. Confucius:

> "In ancient times, men learned with a view
> to their own improvement. Nowadays, men
> learn with a view to the approbation of
> others."

We want to be liked or looked up to by others, even knowing that this is approbation by appearances. Appearances mattered in Confucius's time. They matter nowadays. Liars have always been liars. There are just more of them in a position to lie to us. The constant may be our gullibility. More people may be lying to us under the guise of rationality or of being "scientific," or just generally being more clever media moguls. They become our celebrities and we become their fans. It's still our gullibility that makes the process work. Our marketers have to become better at deceiving us. Otherwise, they would have to tell us the truth, which we wouldn't believe since we know them to be liars. This is from 6th-century B.C. Aesop's *Fables:*

> *"A liar will not be believed, even when he speaks the truth."*

As you may recall, this is from his Fable about "The Shepherd's Boy." The boy was left to watch the flock when they were settling down for the night. The boy called out "Wolf!" three nights in a row, and his family came running but they saw no wolf. The next time he called out "Wolf!" no one came running. He had lied before and caused a great uproar, so they didn't believe him. There actually was a wolf that time, who caused great carnage.

There is the obvious interpretation, which is the moral of the tale. But the boy had never seen a wolf, but in the twilight imagined he was seeing a "wolf." So he was doing what he was told: to call out if he saw a wolf. Another possibility: when he called out "Wolf!" and the others came running, the wolf slinked away, attending to his own survival. Still, the obvious moral could be a good lesson: if you cry "Wolf!" once too often when no wolf is seen by others, you may be labeled as a liar. In that case, when there really was a wolf no one came running, since the boy was not to be trusted as a fill-in shepherd.

That's a good segue into a very common situation. The more complex the delegations in an organization, the less likely what was intended will occur. A competent boss would never delegate a responsible role to an incompetent employee. The delegator needs to know that the person to whom a task is delegated is capable of carrying it out as he or she would. Otherwise, it is going to be carried out according to the understanding and the competence of the person to whom the task is delegated. This often turns out to be a huge problem in large organizations. The top boss delegates a task to one of his or her lieutenants. That person, imagining how busy they like to be seen, delegates the task to one of his or her minions. The person who ends up with the task (which has been interpreted by several other people down the hierarchy) may misunderstand it, or not be competent to carry it out. It happens every day. Whenever a task is kicked down the hierarchy, it changes its meaning. Every person who handles it adds his or her own interpretation. By the time it lands on somebody's plate, it is no longer the task that was required by the top boss. When CEOs complain about their middle managers, this is often at the heart of it.

This was not the moral of Aesop's fable, of course. But, had the boy been forewarned about the dangers (to him) of calling out "Wolf!" when he only *thought* he sighted one? Should he have been capable of handling the situation himself if there was but one wolf? Was he familiar with the proverb "Better safe than sorry"?

Notice also that it doesn't matter if the wolf he thought he saw was real or a figment of his imagination. It is other people who label you as a "liar" either way. Once labeled, it is easy to recall other circumstances to justify the label. What was the covenant made with the boy? Was it about the possibility of a wolf, or the certainty of a wolf?

If a spouse is told about his or her spouse's dalliances, should she or he blame their spouse or the other people – if that spouse had been trustworthy for years? There can be more falsity in gossip than in a person you know.

When do you blame the event and not the person? What was it exactly (in the boy's head) that he had promised? Did he keep *that* promise? Is that more or less important than what you or I assume the promise was?

When you diagnose a situation, do you see it from the point of view of the guilty party, or your own? Where is your guilt in that? What were the boy's relatives' intentions? What was his?

It is easy to understand the lesson if it is pointed out to you. But how are you to understand the "lesson" in the raw, from just the admixture of things that have been told? This was of course Conan Doyle's intention when he invented Sherlock Holmes. How are you to diagnose a situation that has not been pre-diagnosed for you? That was Sherlock's advantage over the criminal – what came to be called Sherlock's Logic. (If interested, take a look at the book, *Sherlock's Logic,* by William Neblett). If you use conventional logic, you will come up with a conventional diagnosis. If you are judging, sometimes you have to deceive others in order to get to the bottom of things. The boy's relatives lost sheep because they didn't respond to his once too often "Wolf!" call. What is it that makes one's judgments right? (There are plenty of people in our prisons who are actually innocent.) When you go along with your fellow-jurors, what makes them right? The film *Twelve Angry Men* explores this conundrum. Or, try Doris Lessing, *Prisons We Choose to Live Inside.* When is it a lie to call a person a liar?

When you are born, your life is a promise. When it is over, your life is a fact. What are the facts that are borne of such promises?

####

We can't know with any certainty what the boy's intentions were. (He is, after all, a fictional character in a story.) We can guess what the author's intentions were because he told us. We can also guess, with some confidence, that the boy's intention was *not* to be called a liar by his people for the rest of his youth. But that's what happened. This opens the door onto a garden of insights about how one's intentions may or may not be realized in the real world.

1. What we encounter there is simply that who you "are" is determined as much by other people as it is by what your intentions may be. By the time you have social intentions, you have already been named, labeled, and known to be who you are by other people. All of us exist as imagined or thought of by other people. It will at the very least be an obstacle to be overcome if you want to impose your own intentions on the social world you have been dropped into. Who you "are" – your identity – will always be some combination of who you think you are (or want to be) and how those other people you co-habit your worlds with believe you to be. Those others judge you and sentence you to being who *they* think you are. If for any reason that doesn't suit you, you are stuck with who *they* have known you to be. That would be the first obstacle you face if you have intentions. It is often the case that the only way you can combat this in real life is to remove those people from your life. To your mother, you will always be her child. Your siblings want you to be who

they have always assumed you to be. Your friends have intentions of their own. One of those might be that you will always be (to them) what you were (to them). These are powerful influences that can easily affect the resolve of your intentions. If you have contrary intentions, your life will always be a struggle to be the determiner and not the victim. The popular culture wants you to be one of the people who has your existence and perpetuity as a fundamental part of who they are. If that doesn't fit your intentions, you have a problem. As Queen Elizabeth I commented:

> *"Create your self-image – or others will create one for you."*

Those are your options. But it is that those others are already operating on the one they have created for you. They have the advantage of getting there before you.

2. In adolescence, you have the opportunity of choosing who are to be your "friends." Your experience in doing so may be fraught with complexities. You would like your friends to be those who will let you be *to them* whoever you want to be. But this is a voluntary relationship (the first in your young life) and neither of you is very experienced at negotiating such a relationship. Those others may have intentions of their own. Each of you wants the other to be who they need the other to be. This doesn't always go well. In Sallust (1st-century B.C.), *The War with Catilene,* we have this observation:

> *"Agreement in likes and dislikes – this, and this only, is what constitutes true friendship."*

Times change. Maybe this is no longer the case. Even so, you will rarely find a strong relationship bud without this as the basis. It is possible for you to like or dislike a person whose likes and dislikes are not in agreement with yours. But that is an exception, and perhaps one that precludes true friendship. Now the problem is given in the following exchange between the greatly distressed Leon Delbecque and Charles de Gaulle from David Schoenbrun, *The Three Lives of Charles de Gaulle:*

> *Delbecque: "General, all of my friends say you are deserting us. They want me to get you to change your Algerian policy. What should I do? De Gaulle: (snapping back): "Change your friends."*

And indeed that is what we sometimes must do. We may intend to keep our faith with old friends. But when they get in the way of newer intentions, we may have no choice but to "change our friends." That may seem fickle. But if your intentions can't be achieved without changing your friends, what *should* you do? When keeping your friends requires you to give up your intentions, which takes priority – your friends or your intentions? Which promise should win out over the other? Balzac wrote:

> *"Friendships last when each friend thinks he has a slight superiority over the other."*

How is that possible? Still, Balzac was a sly old fox. Maybe he was onto something more profound here than mere lastingness. Ralph Waldo Emerson had much to say about friendship. For example, and from his Journal of 1840:

"We are never so fit for friendship as when we cease to seek for it, and take ourselves to friend."

Is he saying that the best friends already have a best friend? Young people seem to need friendship. But when they have learned how to be a friend to themselves, they make better friends. Maybe it is a matter of not being so judgmental, something that one learns when trying to take ourselves to friend. How can you have a perfect friend, when you are not yourself perfect? If you want to know what kind of friends you deserve, look at the friends you've got.

In any event, is one to abandon his or her intentions (as promises) in order to have certain friends, or to abandon the friends one has to further the cause of one's worthy intentions? It's a dilemma that never goes away. When the comfort of friends comes into conflict with your worthy intentions in life, what do you do? If you are not struggling with this dilemma, what dilemmas should you be struggling with?

3. It has often been observed that people who betray their intentions in order to get along socially with other people are the happiest people.

Maybe. It has also been observed over many years and epochs that those who subordinate the ease of socializing to their worthy intentions are the happiest, and the most alive. Can being gregarious be one's best intention in life? Is the choice between being a martyr and an achiever the best choice we can make in our lives? Perhaps the contretemps has to do with the pop culture in which we all imbibe. We can't control it, but we can't be immune to it. It precedes us and it will live on after us. For good or ill, it evolves as if it had a life of its own. It is always a player in everyone's life. It is one's immediate environment. Most people want to be like most people, and that's where they go.

The Greek enclave from which Alexander the Great emerged was known as Macedon (what we would now refer to as Macedonia). It was not so much a place as a culture. It was fiercely opposed to the importation of any larger (Greek?) culture. It was a veiled matriarchal culture. It was the mothers who provided the discipline to raise their sons as warriors. Alexander was the king's son, a warrior brought up by his mother to lead other warriors. It was a highly disciplined, tough upbringing – both intellectually and physically.

Alexander was a brilliant strategist – as everyone who wants to provide leadership must be. He wanted to prove to his mother (and his father) that he could conquer the known world. So he did, by *never* doing what the leaders of those other empires thought he was going to do. He left the conquered administrators in charge. And he brought them many benefits – such as postal service. He kept his promises to them. And he required them to keep their promises to him. As he moved on with his army, he left behind positive relationships, based on their mutual promises. Real promises that will be kept are rare. They must get your attention…If you deserve them.

The main point in all of this is simple, but not always obvious. It is that in order to conquer life, you have to extract yourself from your comfortable routines, guided by the lessons which are the "ruts" derived from habitude, and venture forth into the world you want to make. You do this in order to avoid being made by the world you leave behind. Alexander did not make a name for himself by continuing his own mother's discipline, or his own father's tutelage. He had to leave that world behind in order to change the world as he envisioned it.

No one you or I know is ever likely to change the world we know in that grandiose a way. But the principle remains the same. You have to give up who you are in order to make yourself into who you think you ought to be. You can entertain fantasies about who you want to be. But until you go forth and do what has to be done (in the Epictetus sense), you have no real intention. All you have is a subjective fantasy. There's nothing wrong with that, as long as you acknowledge it as a fantasy and not as an intention. Any real intention carries with it a promise at least to yourself to fulfill your intention. Joshua Bell was not born knowing how to play the violin in front of his critics. Rene Fleming was not born with the voice she has today. LeBron James was not born a basketball star. Those were achievements that came with a conscious intent – a promise to oneself and the world to do what had to be done.

It seems like a simple recipe. One wonders why most people don't see it that way.

> *"First, say to yourself what you would be;*
> *and then do what has to be done."*

8 Your Favorite Hypocrite

A hypocrite at large is possibly no more than a temporary irritation to you. When *you* are the hypocrite, it's more like practicing how to poison yourself from within, a subtle form of long-term suicide.

Adlai Stevenson – who may have been the last politician of principle in America – playfully defined a hypocrite as

> *"...the kind of politician who would cut down a redwood tree, then mount the stump and make a speech for conservation."*

There may be as many definitions of hypocrisy as there are people who practice it – and, as Don Marquis suggested, that would probably be all of us. A hypocrite in this perspective is a person whose pretense is to appear to be X, when in action turns out to be almost the opposite. It is a form of duplicity, but more like a character flaw than a one-off attempt to be duplicitous for gain. It is not so much a lie as a double persona, pretending to be one kind of person while behaving in a very contrary way. And, as Marquis says, who hasn't been hypocritical at one point or another in their lives? In a sense, it is *modus operandi* in our modern culture. Pretense – or appearances – may be far more important in our culture than substance (or principle). So, in that sense, it is what makes our world go 'round. George Bernard Shaw, with his usual insight, wrote:

> *"When there is no religion, hypocrisy becomes good taste."*

When there is no central and binding set of principles to live by, then pretense becomes the MO (as above). In general, modern people are more adept at pretense than at being principled. When pretense is the norm, it is socially risky to be the only person around who asserts worthy principles as the way to live. The baby learns quickly that pretending to "love" his or her mommy gets them what they want. It must be the way to go. The famous journalist Ed Howe wrote:

> *"Half the people who make love could be arrested for counterfeiting."*

It's clever. But it's also profoundly realistic, which Howe seemed to be by principle. He may be saying that making love under the rubric of "love" is a very hypocritical pretense...that seems to work half of the time. What happens to the other half, as someone once said, is that they bumble along in their same old ruts, but miserably. Howe loved to play with words just to see how the meaning changed. We should do the same. By counterfeit, he suggests that half the people profess "love," but do so only to get to what we call the love-*making* part. What they promise is not what they deliver. Their promise was counterfeit. They pretend to "love," but that is only to get what they really want, which might be security, or companionship, or even sex. But you can't get far by offering "security," so you offer "love," which allows the security thing to operate unseen.

You can't have someone arrested for duplicity – unless it involves money or some other material disadvantage (which may be against some law). So they do what everyone else does. They practice their skills as hypocrites – that is, appearing to be the kind of person you fall for, while furthering their own agendas. Commercial advertisers get paid billions for the brands or packages you are seduced into buying. What they say about their products is to seduce you (much like a determined suitor). What they *can* say is legislated only at the far boundaries. They can lie without compunction, just as a favored lover can. They're far better at it than you are. They're professionals. You are merely an amateur. That's why we go there to learn how to become more expert at playing the hypocrite game, in lieu of someone in your social circles who is better at it.

George Bernanos, in his book (English title, *We French*) offers us this provocation to ponder:

> *"Democracies cannot dispense with hypocrisy any more than dictatorships can with cynicism."*

That may make us these days (some things used to be what they were purported to be!) a democratic dictatorship because we are both: cynics and hypocrites.

But, more seriously, what could he have meant by saying that democracies cannot dispense with hypocrisy? Did he mean only that politicians and other functionaries have to be hypocrites? Or did he mean to imply that there is something peculiar about democracies that makes it not only possible but necessary that we all eventually become hypocrites? "Liberated" women seem to do a better job of making hypocrites of their children than oppressed women used to be. Or did he mean that his comments should be taken to apply only to the French? A cynic, it would seem, is someone who doubts the validity of anything other people say or do. Is it the permissiveness that comes with democracies? Is it the freedom to be opinionated without first being well informed about what you are talking about? Is "political correctness" the kind of hypocrisy that is inevitable in a democracy? Are the other militant cults that spring up in a democracy "democratic"? If not, what could have been Bernanos' intentions with his words?

Why would a person be hypocritical unless he or she assumed they could get away with it...to their social or monetary advantage? Are we raised to be hypocrites by the social systems of the pop culture and its values? In his *Table Talk* (1569), Martin Luther had written:

> *"Superstition, idolatry, and hypocrisy have*
> *ample wages, but truth goes a-begging."*

And that was before he died in 1546. There are glimpses of the truth in hypocrisy, but if effective it is obscured by the performance of the hypocrite. So it is not new. It is not modern. It had its beginnings when people first gave up confronting nature and began confronting one another. Truth has never had much of a run in all of human history. That's because we talk, we maneuver, we manipulate. Words are good for everything that is not the truth, if we understand rightly his notion of "ample wages." We create our human worlds in words and meanings. They are not variations on the themes of truth. They are variations on the beliefs of people. A word or a meaningful gesture is a metaphor. In that sense, *we* are metaphors. We are metaphors of how we talk about what we talk about. Our technologies are denials of truth. We are quashing the human spirit. People exist as they become corroborated, not by any truth but by the other people who we in turn corroborate.

From *The Book of Common Prayer,* we ask the good Lord to deliver us –

> *"From all blindness of heart, from pride, from vainglory, and hypocrisy...."*

We need the help of a greater power to keep us from doing what we can't seem to help doing. We are not as perhaps we should be. We are hypocrites, deniers of even the ancient *Tao*. Apparently our strength lies in emulating what other people do and have and are, not in following the path to the good life. We follow the path that has been laid before us by the people we know and the people we know about who have preceded us. It is not people's intention to be good. It is their intention to be like everyone else is. If they are mostly hypocrites, the only choice to be made and still get along in this world is to be the kind of hypocrites they are. Would your best friend be duplicitous for his or her own benefit? Yes.

Would your own parent? Yes. We have some interest in the truths we espouse. Otherwise, we have precious little interest in any truths that we do not harbor. We would rather malign...or even kill, as has happened.

This is what W. Somerset Maugham had to say in his *Cakes and Ale* about the difficulty and the vigilance needed to be as good a hypocrite as anyone you know:

> *"No one can be a humbug for five-and-twenty years. Hypocrisy is the most difficult and*

> *nerve-racking vice that any [person] can*
> *pursue; it needs an unceasing and a rare*
> *detachment of spirit. It cannot, like adultery*
> *or gluttony, be practiced at spare moments;*
> *it is a whole-time job."*

Who could have put it better? He's saying that hypocrisy is not a vice you can pick up or lay aside. It is a habit, developed over time. It is an aspect of a person's lifestyle (if the person is relatively good at it). It is something the person can't help performing, since it has become so much a part of who he or she is. It is a competency which, once mastered, will be utilized – in the sense that we think and do what we have become competent at thinking that way and doing that way. It is a fundamental part of the swamp that envelops us and that we know as our pop culture. It is fashionable and normative. Telling the truth (as a person knows it) is neither fashionable nor normative. All babies we refer to as beautiful, all ugly adults according to their occupations and not their appearance. All road rage is pent up truth. Who should we be enraged at if not ourselves for choosing to be there?

What does Maugham mean when he writes that becoming a passable hypocrite *requires* an unceasing detachment of spirit? Whose spirit is being truncated by hypocrisy? If others are not perturbed by your hypocrisy, why should you care to be thus labeled by them? This whole-time job he refers to may be intended to mean that we take it with us wherever we go, whether to church, to a party, to work, or home. It can't be engaged in and then not engaged in – like an affair. It becomes a habit. And, as we know, *we don't just "have" habits. They have us.* They take us where they go, not where we might intend to go. The kind of ubiquitous hypocrisy he is writing about is not something intentional on our part. It is something we can't help doing because it has become a part of who we are. *Most* people don't shoot other people (it is more likely that their victims will commit suicide, of their own volition). But if misleading other people (duplicity) is not illegal, should it be?

Many people don't have much of a clue about what they want to be when they grow up. So they are easily influenced by their predators, whether by intention or inadvertently. Most people want to think and be and do like most other people. To them, actually doing life is an echo of what their peers are thinking, being, and doing. Life is contagious. Since it is too complicated to think about, we simply copy what others are doing. Hypocrisy is nearly universal, because it is how most of the people you observe and want to be like...live their lives. They probably had no intention of being hypocrites. But if they were dying of a communicable disease, they probably had no intention of doing so. Whatever is going on in your favorite TV programs (including insidious commercial advertising) and the gossip surrounding your favorite celebrities will influence you. If those happen to carry a heavy dose of hypocrisy, you will likely see it as the best way of living your life. You don't become a hypocrite because you intend to. You become a hypocrite because most of the people you encounter in your life are already that way.

In his *Tristam Shandy*, Lawrence Sterne put it to us in this way:

> *"Of all the cants which are canted in this canting world, ...the cant of hypocrisy may be the worst..."*

If you can't guess what Sterne might have meant by cants, canted, and canting, you might not quite have the right sense of what he is saying. A cant (not related to the contraction can't) is a way of causing the world to be askew. The cant of hypocrisy tilts the world in an unfavorable way, which is why it may be the worst in this canting world of ours. For example, if you attend a movie with a friend or two, and if you ask them afterward if they liked the movie, they might grudgingly say "I liked it," or "I didn't like it." This is not a comment about the movie. It is a comment about the speaker – as in "What Peter tells me about Paul tells me more about Peter than about Paul." It is a way of choosing up sides about Paul and thus of bonding together with your friends in the brief discussion. You will like the people who liked the movie if you liked the movie. You will like less the people who said they didn't like the movie if you liked the movie. So if you all want to talk about the movie, the first question was misleading. The next question would be "Why?" Did you like the plot, the themes, the music, the casting, the cinematography, the direction, etc.? Then you would be talking about the movie.

That's how easy it is to fall into the cant of hypocrisy in our pop culture.

Usually, we think of a hypocrite as a person who is duplicitous with other people. We don't often ask how the cant of hypocrisy may be affecting the hypocrite. It's time we did so, because it is the certain effect. The social consequences on the other hand are never quite as certain.

In his *Maxims*, La Rochefoucauld (1665) wrote:

> *"The most trifling disloyalty to ourselves does people far more harm...than the greatest they commit to others."*

We cannot of course ask the author what he meant by that – what he intended to get across to us by that terse statement. But since our interpretation makes us at least the co-author of what we read, let us see where that might take us of real value to our perspective on such things.

- First, to *dissemble* is commonplace, for it is to conceal one's intentions, to fail to tell the truth as one knows it. It is a form of lying, of being disloyal to ourselves, whether intended or not.

- We know this is the way of the world because we were likely brought into this world and brought up by people who dissembled whenever it was in their interest to do so.

- We also know that there are popular card games (and other games popular in our culture) where we can practice and refine our deceits. May the best dissembler win. The game most played by the most people is of course the game of love, from which we have our expression, "All's fair in love and war."

- If you knew what you really needed to know about buying that used car, you might not buy it. So you are stuck with what you can get the seller (or the lover) to divulge.

- So we know that this is merely the social person's MO in life. We can fake out other people for our own benefit.

- But the least often question asked is what does this do to the deceiver – the person who is telling a lie by dissembling?

- One's ability to manipulate others by dissembling may certainly be a social capability that can pay off. But *to be able to deceive others makes it possible to deceive oneself.*

- When one is faking his or her way in poker, it carries with it the ever-present possibility of deceiving oneself. And self-deception is often what gets in the way of one's real intentions. Self-deception is often the primary cause of failure in life, or in one's career.

- Dissemblers – people who are good at lying to others and getting away with it are typically people who are good at lying to themselves, which they can rarely get away with. To misread others may be unfortunate. But to misread oneself may be tragic.

- When you can no longer tell *when* you are and when you are not lying to yourself, you are attacking yourself from the inside—akin to a kind of cancer of the mind. No pain, just a sort of truncation and dissolution of the health of the mind.

- When a hypocrite talks to herself, both voices eventually become hypocritical. It is like a sparring match between two people, both of whom are inflicted with a form of dementia – of Parkinson's if not of Alzheimer's.

- Mental problems are often accompanied by physical ailments of one sort or another, in much the same way that chronic physical ailments (because they interfere with one's lifestyle)...will often produce mental problems.

- So what we are talking about here is not just another psychological problem, but something that can affect one's whole *life* trajectory.

- In other words, becoming a successful hypocrite has some serious unintended consequences. People who are duplicitous (hypocrites) may have to up their game in order to stay in the game. This will, at least by mid-life, begin to take its toll.

- When truth goes a-begging, so does the potential richness of one's life. If hypocrisy is a whole-time job, as Maugham expressed it, then there is precious little time left over for the person's growth and other competencies.

- And what does all of this have to do with *intention*? Mainly, just this: that a person's worthy intentions get at least side-tracked if not obliterated by the kind of thinking required to be a full-time practicing hypocrite. In our world, we have to learn from hypocrites. Since it is normative, you have to be reasonably good at it to be admitted to the social games that make our social worlds go 'round.

- The more attention you have to give to your wayward profession of hypocrisy, the less attention you have to give to other things. Nature gets its due by being abolished. Marriage gets its due by being distorted at the outset. One's life gets its due by being drained of its vigor.

- *To say what you mean, and to mean what you say* is not just a slogan on the margin of your reading or your calendar. It's the only known ameliorative to the spread of hypocrisy. If it is not a warning sign on your dashboard, it should be. Too much is at stake for it not to be – both individually and collectively.

This is the heart and soul of intention (or intentionality). *To say what you mean* requires you to know what you mean because you know what your worthiest intentions are, and that this is what is necessary to move things ahead on a right path. *To mean what you say* requires you to have considered the consequences pro and con (even the potential unintended consequences) and found them efficacious (or not) for everyone's life – including the life of the society. The Navaho had a saying that went something like this:

> Before you open your mouth to say something, make sure that it will perpetuate everyone's apprehension of the beauty in their lives, will keep our truths, and will keep our culture on its rightful path.

To the extent that is a reasonably good paraphrase of what was meant, it may be relevant to our modern lives.

"Free speech" is not free if it disrupts other people's lives, or if it puts one's life or culture on a wrong path.

Hypocrites don't care about any consequences except their own. About this, they have to outdo their competitors. If by their deeds they put their culture on the road to hell, they do not care. They do not have long-term positive consequences in mind. Their concerns begin and end with the process itself. If they can gain an immediate advantage for themselves, they have won the game. But they may have lost by winning the game. If yours is the voice of a hypocrite, your inner voice will eventually become just as hypocritical. Thus you would end up being *your favorite hypocrite.*

The indigenous Indians of America considered their acted-upon intentions to have positive consequences five or six *generations* out. Many people these days apparently cannot do this for their own lifespan. Otherwise they would be able to see that hypocrisy – no matter how normative it is – is a life-threatening disease.

You couldn't ponder all of this without bumping up against the concept of *trust.* You see immediately that it is not a binary thing. In his *Gnomologia: Adages and Proverbs* (1732), Thomas Fuller saw it this way:

> *"It is an equal Failing to trust everybody and to trust nobody."*

You might think that in a world like ours, you would be better off to trust nobody. But that, Fuller says, is a failing equal to trusting everybody. In his more recent

The Disrespectful Dictionary, Victor Cahn defined "trust" as follows:

"Trust, v. To lay oneself open to deception."

It is only the people you trust who can deceive you. It is only the persons who are closest to you who can betray you. Some level of trust is a necessary condition of any relationship. Now you have the relationship (e.g., a marriage or a partnership), but it is only those with whom you have a relationship who can most readily deceive you, or betray you. The most vulnerable person in a kingdom was the King, or Queen. The quickest path to kingship was to murder the king (even if that were your own father). That doesn't happen often in modern times. But there is more than one way to depose the ruler. We do it every day in our organizations, and once in a while to our presidents. We just use modern means and modern euphemisms when we do so. JFK was assassinated. But so was Nixon. Nothing much has changed, except the words we use to explain it.

If you can't trust your President, whom can you trust? If you can't trust yourself, doesn't that leave you fairly helpless in a world you never made? A lot of people trusted their banks back in 1929. That didn't keep those banks from closing. A lot of people these days trust their horoscopes. That doesn't keep those prognostications from being wrong. A lot of people trust the weather forecasts. But that doesn't keep them from being wrong. After a check-up, your doctor may say you're in great shape and will live a long life. But that doesn't guarantee that you won't die on the way home. Scientists trust their probabilities. But that doesn't mean they know what is going to happen, or when.

Trust is a tricky word. As a word, it doesn't do anything. If you trust your car to start and it doesn't, are you any better or worse off than if you hadn't trusted at all? Given a situation, what part did *trust* play? Were the gods invented by humans to have someone to blame for bad fortune, and someone to praise for good? Is trust a way of garnering certainty in an uncertain world? If so, are we missing something vital in our perspective on our worlds? We know that parents and other soothsayers cannot be trusted to predict the future in a world with as much randomness as we are exposed to. (I.e., "bad" kids can turn out to be good, and "good" kids can turn out badly). Can we trust the *implications* of what the famous biologist D'Arcy Thompson said? --

> *"Things are the way they are because they got to be that way."*

Is that a useful premise for living the good life – that things happen, that it is impossible to control *everything*? Or that it is impossible to take the uncertainty out of everything, as seems to be our intention? Is the best perspective the one that says you must trust yourself – that if you are trustworthy that will optimize your life? To bet on yourself might require you to be far more competent as a human being than you are. Who's going to go there, if there is the possibility that you can, in fact, trust a god invented by people?

Such questions do not have answers beyond our own trust in our own perspectives and methods. Those are perennial. There is a Russian proverb (are these the best we can do?) that suggests the answer has more to do with faith than with fact:

"Trust in God but look to yourself."

This resonates with the Arab saying: *"Trust in God but tie your camel."* There is trust and then there is prudence – operating in the real world according to what goes on there.

If you are a good reader (most people aren't), your takeaways from this chapter might be:

- That if you follow the crowd and become a hypocrite (lessons abound in the media and likely in your neighborhood), you will gradually lose your immunity to being deceived by others. That's because you might imagine that you know all the tricks. You may have known some of the current tricks yesterday. But today is another day.

- When you get good enough to fake yourself out, you may be setting yourself up for failure at this basic normative game of everyday life. You become so tricky that you trick yourself out.

Perhaps the best you can do if you're on that track is to contemplate the implications of one of *Murphy's Laws – Bralek's Rule for Success:*

> *"Trust only those who stand to lose as much as you when things go wrong."*

So what do you do when your main advisor in such things is you? If you had adopted the right *intentions* in the first place, you wouldn't be faced with that dilemma, would you?

9 Remember the Future, Forget the Past

Between cameras, memories, and the pop culture, it may be hard to comprehend the thoughts above in their stark form. But by the end of this chapter, you will be able to see not only the remarkable perspective this provides you, but its empirical validity. No matter how we are reminded of it all the time, living in the past leads to being imprisoned by the past. We should want to have such an imperative relationship with the *future*.

All intentions are forward looking. Unless you have some sort of mental deficiency, it must be obvious that you do not have intentions with respect to your past. The past is done. No one has much of a future there. It may be fun to track your ancestors. They did indeed contribute to the world you live in. But you can't really change much about your past – except for your interpretation of it, which can have a unique contribution to who you think you are. But if you have worthy intentions, they have to be about your future, not your past.

Your habits of thinking, being, and doing that precede you in this world of ours become weightier the older you become. If you have no intentions with respect to your future existence, then you will be a puppet of that weightier past, simply because there is more of it than there is of your future. Our pop culture leads us to assume that our pasts are more important than our futures. This is often so, even though the past is not something in which we can live, and the future is. Our habits, our routines, and our relationships with the people we know and the possessions and things we are familiar with want us not to change. They want us to be who and how we were yesterday. They constitute our status quo. And our personal status quo can be tyrannical when there is a threat of any path ahead except the one we are on.

Our past is like a prison. It wants to keep things as they *were*, not as they could be. You have to escape the tyranny of the past in order to have any hope that your intentions will make any difference in your life.
People cannot live their lives in the past – except in their imaginations. Any actual life has to be had in the fleeting present or your intended future. Unless you think you have no future, the only life you can have is the one that you intend to have in the future.

Still not convinced? Try being alive in your past. You can think about it, you can fantasize it. But you can't actually be alive in your past. You can only do that in your future. So if you were to contemplate changing your life in any way, you would have to do that in your future. If you don't care, neither does any future that might happen to come your way. And why is it so difficult to change things in the present? For the simple reason that the present is like a knife-edge. As soon as you think about it or talk about it, it becomes the past. And the past exists in how you imagine it. It has no other existence. It is yours to interpret in any way you are capable of. But it has no other actual people in it. You may have some memory of it. But you can't share that with them. Others may have some memory of it. But they can't share that with you. There are no live people in anyone's memories of the past. They are only there as we recollect them. And our recollections are notoriously fictional. We don't work from any stored or archived memories. It is a creative process – altogether as creative as imagining the future.

We remember the future in the same way we remember the past – in our imaginations (which is where those experiences may mainly exist in the first place). We imagine the details of our experiences. We may imagine we share those experiences. But we don't because we can't. We can only describe them to one another. We can't have the same one someone else has. They can't have the same one we have. So the past is not as "real" as a movie is. We can share the "same" movie, but not anyone's interpretation of it. We can have the same parents, but our personal *experiences* of them and with them will be different. The past is not an actual series of events. It will vary with the perspectives of the person. Even historians know that what happened in the past will vary with the historian doing the telling. Custer could not have had the same story to tell about his encounter with Sitting Bull's warriors that was told by those warriors who were successful there. There are always at least two histories of any war: the winners' and the losers'. It is the same with any love affair or its history. There is always a differing perspective. For people, the past is made up of those differing perspectives, not so much of indelible events. History itself is just a way of explaining things that differs from culture to culture, person to person, and historian to historian.

There are no living people in your *memory* of the past. It is all in the way you imagine it was. Probably with tongue in cheek, Franklin Adams quipped:

*"Nothing is more responsible for the good old
days than a bad memory."*

Beyond the chuckle he had undoubtedly intended, he is
reminding us that everyone's past is reconstructed. It is
a creative act, not simply an act of remembering. There
is no videotape of your past, no "facts" at all beyond
possibly some geographical ones. And even those get
colored over depending on who we are talking to. So
on the serious side, this can also serve to remind us
that how we reconstruct our pasts can be good for our
present and future lives, or bad. The people in a photo
exist only like a race card exists in a photo. They are
merely images. All the rest of it has to be supplied by the
viewer – who they are, what they meant to you, the story
line that precedes or follows. A selfie is not *you*. It is an
image of someone. All the rest of its meaning you supply.

So our photos and videos may be stepping stones to our
pasts. But in concocting the meaning of any past you
may or may not have had, you are supplying the story
lines and any meaning they may have for you in the
present. We don't remember the past. We re-create it
from our perspective in the present. You can make the
story of your past one that is good for your life in the
present and the future, or bad for your life in the present
and the future. There are people who regret something
they did or said in the past. There are some people who
are victimized by how they remember their past. In his
Journal of 19 June 1838, Emerson wrote:

"Be not the slave of your own past."

What Emerson was getting at here is the early days of a
universal belief (brought on mainly by pop psychology

and scientism) that the past *determines* the present. If you believe that, you would have trouble believing in one of our commonest experiences of "love," since the motive for love is *something expected in the future*. That implies that the future can as readily carry the motive for one's present perspective on his or her world as can the past. To be a "slave of your own past" intimates that the *story* you harbor of your past is the kind of story that makes it mandatory you continue that story into your present and often even your future. It means that the story of your past is one that *mandates* you to continue living in that story until you die. That's the kind of slavery Emerson was eluding to. Novels worked that way. The coming of the movies would work that way. Gossip especially worked that way. If someone were behaving in a way you would not expect, given who you imagined that person to *be,* you would assume there was something wrong with the person and not with the norm by which you were measuring that person. People's lives are supposed to make sense, to that person as well as to all the rest of us. When Emerson is warning us not to be the slave of our own past, he is also saying that (if we are that slave), this becomes a serious barrier to having and/or enacting any intentions we may have that don't provide the expected continuity of the story of our own lives to that point. In other words, if our intentions don't seem consistent with who we imagine we are, they can readily get us into trouble with ourselves and with those who presume to know us. And, indeed, this is what can happen.

More than half of the adults in our society report some vague dissatisfaction with who they are. They may want to be different than who they "are." But this is impeded at the outset by the constraints of continuity. Any change has to be minor, and has to make sense to us *and* to anyone who purports to know us. If it doesn't make sense, then it is simply unlikely to become an intention of that person, or to be acted upon. You are not free to have or to act upon your intentions if they seem inconsistent with who you are. If you have ever wondered why people who are unhappy with who they are don't just change, that's the reason.

Ogden Nash had a little ditty about this in his *You Can't Get There from Here:*

> *"One thing about the past,*
> *It is likely to last.*
> *Some of it is horrid and some sublime,*
> *And there is more of it all the time."*

We keep our pasts alive in our photos, recordings, memories, and conversations. So they are likely to "last." And they are mixed, as they would be since we were only learning how to be somebody. There is more of our past as we age. The trajectory gets longer, day by day. Does the future shrink? Only for some people. There are some people who live intentionally all their lives. So he's writing about the average, the normative. That may include you and me.

In his *Look Back in Anger,* John Osborne wrote about these same backward-looking people:

> *"They spend their time mostly looking forward to the past."*

The past, for so many people, is a place of refuge. People go there to escape the meaninglessness of their lives in the present and for certain in their future. Some people give up even having a future. They no longer have intentions. They just try to deal with whatever comes their way. They vote for whichever politician promises the most for them. They are a burden to themselves and on their society. *It is having worthy intentions and acting on them that unburdens self and society.* If you've ever been to the average "retirement" home, you have witnessed their plight. You will see people there who didn't live their intentions, and they don't have the energy or the will to start now.

For want of an intention in life, a life was lost.

For want of that life, a society may take a wrong turn.

The well-known novelist Jessamyn West perhaps said it best in the fewest words in her novel, *The Life I Really Lived:*

> *"Faithfulness to the past can be a kind of death above ground."*

That is metaphorically speaking, of course. (But is there any other kind of speaking?) We explain things, and then we're stuck with living the explanations concocted by previous generations – and our progeny with ours. About "faithfulness," she means something like feeling compelled to perpetuate the story of your life much as you had construed it from the outset. Our pop psych culture encourages us to think that we have a "self" – an identity – which comes from the past and which we must be faithful to. When she compares that kind of faithfulness to the past as a kind of death above ground, she is referring of course to the kind of death we suffer while still alive – "above ground." We become increasingly dead to our futures, where being fully alive is at least possible. Echoing Emerson, she sees this faithfulness to the past as a kind of slavery to that past, even though our lives are in the future. There is no life in the past. It may be popular to be faithful to our pasts. But in our interpretations of our pasts, there is no guarantee that doing so is in any way healthy or hygienic. To perpetuate our pasts is not necessarily where our future lives come from.

You have heard older people say when confronted with the need to change their perspective in some minor way: "It's the way I have always been. I can't change now." That's the death above ground that West is talking about. When people are faithful to their pasts rather than their futures, they began to die and wither on the vine. The best life comes from how you invent your past in telling your story about it, and what your intentions are for the future.

So we may need to explicate the title of this chapter somewhat. Again, metaphorically, we don't mean that it is either possible or efficacious to "forget the past." Just because the past increases in mind share as the future perhaps decreases, that doesn't compel you to give it more weight in your life. We have our dreams about the future. We also have our dreams about the past. We should *strategically* forget those aspects of our lives that do not fit our dreams about one's future. The past is just as forgettable as is the future. You want to make your future memorable. To do so, you may have to forget those aspects of your past that don't contribute to your future being. Like a movie editor, you need to take out of the movie what does not contribute to making it compelling with regard to its trajectory. It is not a matter of taking out what is not true vs. what is, but of reinterpreting your past life to fit as background for your present and future life. It is treating your past as if it were just fiction, just as we often treat our futures as if they were just fiction – because they are. Your life is a story. You need to author that story as best you can to represent the worthiness of your having been here. An author doesn't need someone to provide any factual past. The author does so to make the story plausible.

That's what "Forget the Past" is intended to mean. Now, what is the strange phrase, "Remember the Future" supposed to mean? In crafting the story of your life in your imagination, you want it to end in some meaningful way. You may have forgotten that aspect of your youth when you wanted your life to make a difference. You wanted a legacy that represents you as you would want to be remembered. That's all in the future. If you want to be remembered in a meaningful way, you have to compose the story of your life from start to finish to make that happen. Thus you have to strategically "forget" your past, and just as strategically to "remember" your future." As C. S. Lewis was appropriately quoted as saying:

> *"You can't go back and change the beginning,*
> *but you can start where you are and change* ✓
> *the ending."*

You can't change the past. But you can avoid becoming its slave by reinterpreting it to fit your chosen future. That's remembering the future in order to fictionalize a past that would justify in a dramatic way that future. Forgetting the past requires you to escape being its victim.

If you can remember the future that will characterize you as you want to be remembered, it becomes possible.

(Does it help to be reminded that all intentions are about the future?)

You can have intentions for the future, but not for the past. The past may help you to understand certain things about your present. But it may not help you to understand your future. That must be *made* – if not by you then by whatever happens to you along the way. The famous British legislator Edmund Burke (in a letter to a member of the French National Assembly) commented:

> *"You can never plan the future by the past."*

Unlike so many of our modern politicians, Burke was very articulate. He thought his peers were often plodding down the wrong track and he told them so. What he is suggesting here to a French peer is that taking the past as a lesson for the future solves no problems and illuminates no path for future planning. What he is suggesting is that the past, however interpreted by people, is a faulty basis for planning any future. The implication of his comment is that the future should be made by principle and by intention, not by however the past is viewed. It would be safe to say, given his context, that we cannot let the past dictate the future. He was a pragmatic idealist. The past may reveal some lessons that would have been useful in the past. If faced with inventing your future, you should never use the past as a template for doing so. You need to forget the past in order to remember better the future you have envisioned. You need to remember your intentions for the future to avoid becoming a slave of your past.

The well-known and influential industrialist Charles Kettering had a very concise perspective on the future:

> *"My interest is in the future because I am going to spend the rest of my life there."*

One could be well rewarded in the future by taking a moment to reflect on this observation.

We are *all* going to spend the rest of our lives in the future. And yet so few people have that kind of interest in it. That's a bit like saying that people are going to spend eternity in hell, but their being indifferent to that prospect. Given how furiously people spend their present, that should come as no surprise. We live in a time when most people seem to have little interest in the past, and less interest in the future. The age of "narcissism" seems to leave people adrift in the present with its fads and fashions. There is something about the "ME!" generation that makes it easy to forget the past, but to have no reason to remember their intentions with respect to the future if, indeed, they had any that lasted beyond a day or two. In other words, Kettering's observation would seem to have little interest to them. If it has little interest to you, it could be because you have no intentions about where you are going to spend the rest of your life. As Alexander Pope wrote in his *An Essay on Man* :

> *"Not one looks backward, onward still he goes, Yet ne'er looks forward further than his nose."*

Or, this American graffito (1980s) seems to capture the spirit of our age:

> *"Due to a lack of interest tomorrow has been canceled."*

Not much new there. Pope was writing in 1734. We don't seem to weary of the same-o.

A quip from the quipster Evan Esar may be appropriate here:

> *"What the future has in store for you depends largely on what you place in store for the future."*

There is not the same future for everyone and anyone who arrives there. The future means different things to different people, depending not upon the future but upon the person who thinks about it, talks about living the rest of his or her life there, or is indifferent to it. In other words, the future is person-specific, just as that person's intentions are person-specific. What those intentions mean is what they mean to that person. Who you *are* determines what the past or the future means...to you. The future that you will be living in the rest of your life is the one you *remember* when you get there tomorrow. Like your life, it is what you make of it, not what "it" is. So the future is just like the past: they both exist in how we talk about them, in what they mean to us. Escaping the tyranny of your past makes it possible for you to invent the future as you would have it. The future is not some mystical place way off in time and place. It is tomorrow... your tomorrow. That's your future. The question is: How will you remember it today?

####

It's not easy to forget or to reinterpret the past (as we have discussed earlier). The sheer weight of it makes it seem imperative. It takes considerable courage to make the future equal in mindshare. But if that is where you are going to spend the rest of your life (as Kettering said), it makes good pragmatic sense to remember the future at least as much or more than you remember your past. What you remember about the future are your intentions. If your intentions are worthy...and *if* you are committed to them...then remembering your future will command as much or more mindshare than has your past. There are two reasons why most people don't remember the future in this way:

1. They don't harbor *any* intentions, or if they do, it may be that their intentions are not worthy enough for them to commit to. A person who intends to win a gold medal at the Olympics may have no problem preparing herself physically and mentally for the competition she will encounter when the games are on. The difference between that person and the rest of the wannabes is that they don't (or can't) make that sort of commitment to their own future. A person who has no desire to mingle with the educated is likely to look upon them negatively. A person who has no worthy aspirations for her or his future will always have a ready excuse.
2. The other reason is that they have no passion for their future. They are content to hang back and see what the future brings *to them*. Most people do not live passionately in love with their purposes in life. They are willing to be passive and to adapt to whatever comes along.

Passion is ineluctable. It gives the person no option but to pursue his or her passion. If it is to last, it has to be refueled. Our passions are blind. They move us to action, but with no guarantee that such action will be beneficent. There is a Greek saying that captures well the part that our passions play in our lives:

"Rule your passions or they will rule you."

They are the energizing force, not the navigational force. They will speed you on your way, but they cannot advise you about whether or not your way is the way you ought to be on. Like all drivers, they provide what they provide. They have no conscience. You are the one who is supposed to have a conscience. You may be passionate about your cause. But unless your cause is a worthy cause, you cannot justify the outcome no matter how passionate you were about your cause. What does it mean that if you do not rule your passions, they will rule you? It means that your passions will lead you out of control if you do not rule them. Your passions may lead you to "road rage." But they will not share the outcome with you. You may say that the devil (your passions) made you do it (assault or mayhem). But your passions will not do time (in prison or in hell) for your transgressions under their influence. Your intentions may matter. Your passions may not. If they did, it might be sort of like claiming innocence by reason of DUI. Passion is almost the opposite of rationality – today the reigning perspective. In the modern world, to be rational is to be sane. To be driven by passion would make you "insane" – out of control, unreasonable. The passions of our great poets and composers have not infrequently been thought of as their marginal insanity. This is probably little more than one of many semantic pitfalls in our pop culture. It may be, as Szasz and others have argued, that those who are labeled "insane" may be the sane ones, the rest of us being insane. "The rest of us" being too ready to adapt to an insane world.

This is not intended to mean that you have to be insane to be driven to startling artistry in any field. It only means that a life without passions isn't much of a life. You may be misunderstood. But who can readily understand what one person you know sees in another (something that you can't see) that they should fall in love and maybe even get married? And maybe even have children with whom they can create family problems? What's the sanity in that?

Back to the beginning of all this: "Forget the past" is obviously intended as a metaphor. Metaphors can have a host of literal exceptions. That's because metaphors are not literal – not to be taken literally.

Of course you would not want to forget how to ride a bicycle or drive a car or surf the internet or the TV. You would not want to forget how to swim or how to play the piano. You would not want to forget the skills by which you make a living, or the basics of how to cook or brush your teeth. Nor would you want to forget how to get to the dentist's office if you didn't brush your teeth. There are lots of things that your memory is good for – that you wouldn't *want to* forget, especially if you suffer from Alzheimer's. It's all about *strategic* forgetting.

That's what we are referring to here. What we *are* referring to is why you believe your past determines who you are in the present, or who you will be in the future. There may be something to be said for such prognostications. But there are warning signs everywhere along the way that your belief may be hazardous to the quality of your life.

As Kettering said, he is keenly interested in the future because that's where he is going to spend the rest of his life. That's where all of us are going to spend the rest of our lives. That's one point: that any intentions we may have are intentions about the future. If you have any intentions for your life – at any age – those intentions have to do with your future life, not your past life. Intentions produce anticipation. And it is easy to see that anticipating your future can be far more life-producing than can being enslaved by your past. All anticipation is gone when you are accounting for your life in terms of your past.

In a television interview in the 1980s, Abraham Heschel spoke of *building one's life as if it were a work of art,* in a book entitled *I Asked for Wonder* edited by Samuel Dresner. That analogy speaks to the issue of anticipation. It takes a heap of discipline to make a work of art: beginning with a disciplined imagination about the finished product, the skills and techniques to make something worthy out of a piece of canvas or a lump of clay with the tools at hand, and the self-criticism required to be relentless in the pursuit of the finished product. Above all, perhaps, it takes that disturbing level of dissatisfaction that comes with intention but is eased only by the finished product. Talent alone doesn't mean much. We all have the requisite talent to make and remake our lives. That requires giving up who we are in order to become who we need to be. And then one needs the persistence in spite of any and all problems to see it through. It's easier to make a work of art than it is to make a work of art of one's life.

Why? Because if you want to see the world differently, you have to abandon the perspectives on the basis of which you presently see it (as who you are). In order to see the world differently, you have to be someone other than who you are. An artist doesn't strive for years to get his or her viewers to see the world as he or she sees it. Serious artists strive to get their viewers, through their work, to see the world differently and (for different reasons) *better* – enriching the perspectives and thus the lives of those who apprehend their work.

As we have brushed up against this earlier: perhaps the book that best illuminates this process is by Saint-Exupery. He was one of the earliest for-hire aviators, and one of our most endearing authors – as in *The Little Prince*. He kept the manuscript in his cockpit at all times. It was there when his plane crashed and he was killed. In this book, the French title was *Citadel*, meaning *the mind*, where everyone has their perspectives on things, and thus their inner home. The English version is entitled *The Wisdom of the Sands*. In it, the great desert chieftain tries to "teach" his son how to become a great desert chieftain. More than any other book I know of, it exposes us to how difficult this is (perhaps impossible). It isn't that the son doesn't want to learn. He does. But he does not understand the nuances that his father brought to every example. He doesn't understand the context and how to think about it because he was not his father. He was merely his father's son. We can make thousands of books about how to think about things, about how to do things, about how to be someone. But information is not wisdom. Our educational system is flawed at the outset. Information (or knowledge) is not wisdom. As a commodity to be bought or sold, it becomes objective. But wisdom is subjective. It is personal, not impersonal or even interpersonal. Wisdom (as Siddhartha said) is not communicable. It was the desert chieftain's intention to pass on his wisdom to his son. It may not have been his son's intention to acquire it.

To make of one's life a work of art requires your being an artist. An artist is willing to abandon who he or she is in order to accomplish what has to be accomplished in the real world. That requires being someone else, not doable by any of what we call knowledge. It means that all actions come from who one *is*, not solely from what one knows.

So the second, more important point to be garnered here is that what you can accomplish in the real world comes from who *you* are. It isn't just that you have to make of your life a work of art. It is what does your work of art mean to you? And is it potent enough to give you escape velocity from who you are, and the imagination to remake yourself into who you would need to be?

It is not just forgetting your past. It is *strategically* forgetting certain memories of your past in order to create a different *story* from here on. You have to forget what doesn't justify the story of your chosen future, and replace it with what does. In other words, the story line has to extend from the future into the past. Remember the future and forget the past – that past that doesn't fit the story that gets you there. Tell your story the way the future demands, not the way the past demands.

In "Living Is—" a part of his *Grooks*, Piet Hein wrote:

> *"Living is*
> *a thing you do*
> *now or never—*
> *which do you?"*

10 Intention: the Pathways of Life

Near the end of the last chapter, we saw how it was the desert chieftain's compulsive intention to pass on to his son the wisdom needed to be a great desert chieftain. It was his son's on and off intention to acquire that wisdom. But, like all communication, it doesn't always happen with the results you intended. We map our lives by our intentions. Ships and planes (and automobiles) don't get to where they're going because someone simply *intended* to go to this or that destination. There is always the *how* – and the when and the why and those people who get entangled in our intentions, or we in theirs. How our conscious lives are woven out of our intentions is the process of our interest in this chapter. Our intentions do not come to us with instructions for their implementation. We have to provide those, as we may or may not be capable. That's how our lives get structured by what we do about our intentions. The infant wants to get to somewhere else from where she is. Unable yet to walk, she crawls or scoots. There are always multitudes of ways of becoming cognizant of our intentions, and of fulfilling them.

The desert chieftain, in Saint-Exupery's book, assumed there was only one way to impart his wisdom to his son, and that was to "teach" him the lessons he had learned. If his son had been that interested, he would have asked his father and thus created a mentoring relationship – which *might* have been more effective. How would we know? That is not the process used by the desert chieftain in the story as it was told.

We are always and ever creating the story of our lives. Other's intentions do not necessarily get a hearing there. And it is their lives that most interest *them* – not ours. Why would someone else be keen to further *our* intentions, when they are busy fulfilling their own? Since the worlds involved are those of the mind, and since minds are created and maintained (or not) primarily by the meanings people can lend to those words, we thus arrive at the first lesson in Saint-Exupery's story:

> *If the person you are talking to has not asked you the question to which your comments are the answer, that person will not – cannot – fully understand what you are saying.*

The part that questions play in our lives is profound. Others cannot fully understand you unless you are answering their questions. You can't fully understand me unless I am responding to *your* questions. In a somewhat perverse way, this makes all human understandings hinge on the *curiosity* of the person involved. If you are curious about something in nature, you will ask nature the question and nature will give you the answer. If you are curious about another person, you will ask her the questions you would like the answer to. It would then be your intention to pay attention and get the answers you wanted no matter how many subsequent questions you have to ask. In love, each is the answer to the other's questions. If you are curious about how to become a great desert chieftain, you will ask the questions that bring you the answers you need. If you are curious about how *this* book, for example, can be useful to you in your life, ask "it" the questions you need to ask. Then "its" answers will fulfill *your* curiosity.

That's how understandings are built. In love, each person is the answer to the other person's questions, literally raised or not. (Otherwise, the "magic" doesn't work.) For the desert chieftain's son to really understand his father's pronouncements, he would need to ask the questions for which those pronouncements are the answer. Merely to try to "teach" his son how to be a great desert chieftain (which is deductive), he needed first to answer his son's questions (which is inductive). If the son can't raise those questions, that is evidence of his intention and thus his interest. The ancient Greeks knew this well:

> *"You cannot confer a benefit on an unwilling person."*

That also applies to an *incapable* person. Try it if you are curious, and you will understand. You cannot, even with the best teaching skills there are, talk somebody who is stupid into suddenly being smart.

So what we gather with our questions is never any better than the questions we ask. Could the desert chieftain's son ever ask the great questions to which the father's wisdom might well be the answer? We will never know, because that is not in the story.

So a lesson we may want to draw from Saint-Exupery's story is that *your* story will lead you to certain questions and certain wisdoms, and that someone else's story will lead them to certain other questions and certain other wisdoms. The desert chieftain in Saint-Exupery's story would not have any trouble "talking shop" with another great desert chieftain. But that is not who he is talking to. If the son has no propelling questions to ask, his father's preaching will carry little of interest. It may be that the son's intentions have to do with training his pony, and not himself being trained by his father. If the son's upbringing has not made him curiousabout how his father can achieve what he achieves, his intentions may take him elsewhere. The penultimate question for the father is: why would he want to have a successor who does not want to exceed him, or even to succeed him? And, for the son: why would you want to acquiesce to your father's intention rather than to your own? You cannot "teach" someone how to be a world-class pianist or athlete. You could teach them the skills and whatever else they might *need* to know. As the eminent British management guru Charles Handy has said:

"You can know everything there is to know about management, and still be a lousy manager."

The lesson for the great desert chieftain then may be: *You can teach your son everything there is to know about being a great desert chieftain, but he may still be a lousy chieftain.* The lesson for you is...?

As we talk about it in the modern world, "knowledge" does not refer to know-how. It is an abstract explanation of something or other – intended to have no particular relevance to your immediate world. It is a commodity bought and sold. There are books made up of it. There are occupations based upon it (e.g., college professors, third-grade teachers, and IT "experts"). By-and-large, the "knowledge" which these people and others use and sell to students and clients have little to no relevance to making a good or right life. Physicians and financial advisors are also, like the rest of us, social/biological creatures. They need to know what *they need to know* in order to get by in the world. The "knowledge" they claim to have that makes them feel superior often has nothing to do with the real world they, and all the rest of us, have to live in. If they want to ride a bicycle to work, they might have to know how to ride a bicycle.

Ultimately, their expertise is based on a specialized *argot,* which they always use to talk to each other, and sometimes to bamboozle the rest of us. An argot is the specialized language or jargon used by a group to distinguish them from previous groups or classes or currently-competitive groups. Young people will invariably develop their own argot, to distinguish themselves from the previous generation. The more occupational groups there are, the more argots there will be. Golfers have an argot they use to distinguish who's one of them from those who speak skiing. Children who have imaginary friends will speak to that imaginary friend differently than they do to their parents or to their peers in general. The argot spoken by physicians to one another creates an obstacle to communication with a patient (who speaks in other tongues). And vice versa. A patient who cannot speak the physician's jargon inadvertently establishes an obstacle to their communication. There have always been "secret" languages, intended to keep out those who do not belong, and hang out a welcome mat to those who do. Every occupational group has its own slang, understood by them but somewhat opaque to others who don't belong. A stylized handshake is part of an argot.

Belonging is a way of facilitating communication, whereas being able to identify those who do not belong is a way of maintaining exclusivity. We are herd animals. But it makes a difference to us which herd we belong to, as every juvenile human and every dolphin knows. You can't belong to locker room hilarity unless you know what is funny to those who are there.

####

All of the above is *intended* to be useful background for what comes next. If it isn't, where does the fault lie?

One of the most remarkable aspects of *intentions* in our daily lives is as follows:

If something captures our attention, it is because the person or the object or the idea or the event played a role in some intention of ours in our remembered past, our imagined but fleeting present, or our imagined future. What we pay attention to marks the limits of our lives. If we have no intentions beyond those by which we merely maintain who we are, our lives become thereby petty and stultified. It is having intentions that take us out of our comfort zones, that enrich and enlarge our lives. And *it is via our intentions* (past, present, & future) *that our attention is directed*. Ortega Y Gasset said it perhaps most intriguingly:

> *"Tell me to what you pay attention and I will tell you who you are."*

We become what we pay attention to. And what we pay attention to depends subtly but ineluctably upon our intentions (alive or dead). There is another thought by Ortega that may be useful here:

> *"Our firmest convictions are apt to be the most suspect, they mark our limitations*

and bounds. Life is a petty thing unless it is moved by the indomitable urge to extend its boundaries."

And we extend its boundaries by our intentions. That indomitable urge is not to extend life's boundaries. It is to venture into the world with the courage of your worthy intentions. When people know enough to get by in their small worlds, they are apt to descend into knowing and autopilot rather than continued curiosity. What anyone "knows" does not guarantee a good or worthy life. The key to life is in learning – for example, leaning what you need to know in your circumstances and in your social environment to pursue your worthy intentions. And to *grow*. No "urge" by itself is going to get you there. You have to have the habits of being curious about anything that might bear upon your intentions, and learning what you need to know to fulfill any worthy intentions you may have. Ortega is saying that what you know marks your limitations and your bounds. If you are always learning what you need to know, you are growing – you are growing beyond your current limitations and bounds. In that growth you are being turned on to life, to having a larger, richer life, even to being more alive.

To live fully, you don't need convictions. You need curiosity, and the imaginativeness to pursue your questions wherever they lead you beyond your present bounds and limitations. We have already discussed the role that expectation plays in life. If you have expectations, they are all in your future. You can no longer have expectations about your past...or present. Any expectations you may have are there because you have some *intentions* with respect to your future. If you have no expectations with respect to your future, your life will be made of whatever happens to happen. You will be a product of randomness. Intention is intended to take some of the utter randomness out of your life. The opposite of intention is victimization – either by other people or by the events that occur.

The main point here is that you are continuously being led – either by your intentions, someone else's intentions, or by the random happenings of the day.

The second lesson (somewhat subtler) we may want to draw from all of this is that it is what you pay attention to that puts you on this or that path in your life. If it is something (or someone) you hadn't expected, your attention will be diverted. Some people are led mainly by their intentions. Other people by their diversions. Both are led by what they are paying attention to. If they are being led by their intentions, they are in charge of who they become. If they are being led mainly by their diversions, it will be their diversions that determine who they become. What we pay attention to, as we have seen, is something that has some unique *meaning* to us at that moment. We are attracted to what we think has some meaning for us. If something has captured our attention but we don't know what it is supposed to mean to us, we may be experiencing a moment of growth in our perceptual/conceptual purview. The more you expose yourself to people or things that are not a part of your familiar everyday life, the more possibilities there are for growth. And as we know:

Learning = growth, and growth = life.

In other words, you live fully only when you are learning something new, something that changes your perspective on the world you inhabit. That leads to your growth, and the growth of your mind brings with it the growth of your life. We all grow in direct proportion to how curious we are about the world we live in – no matter how familiar it is. In fact, it is going beyond one's oft-used algorithms that provide growth – growth of spirit, of meaning, and of one's relationship with the world one inhabits.

Your body begins to deteriorate at around the age of thirty. But your mind can continue to grow until you die. That is the best measure we have of quality of life. Not that many years ago, an American (farmers') saying was:

More things rust out than wear out.

The epidemic of dementia in the modern world may be a partial function of just that: of the mind (and sometimes the body) slowly rusting out as a result of lack of stimulation, use, growth. There are always biological/physiological factors. But there are also *always* psychosocial factors in any debilitation of mind or body. One can do little about an aging body, even though it is more likely to mirror the images and the explanations of the pop culture than any ideal model. But, again, the mind (like the brain) is the most plastic of all of life's support functions.

The more it is used, the more it grows. And the more it grows, the more life its owner will have. It grows in what is meaningful to it.

So what is likely is that intentions rule. The worthier (the more efficacious) they are, the better the life of the person. As Abraham Lincoln once quipped (paraphrased here):

> *I guess the only difference between a happy person and an unhappy person is that the happy person has decided to be happy.*

That decision was an *intention*. That no matter what happens, the happy person will be who she intends to be: happy – or at least seeing the silver lining and not the gloom in things. That all-encompassing intention is what the person intends to live by. So she nourishes the habits needed to meet the world that way.

People who are happy do not "blame" their circumstances for being so. But it seems that people who are unhappy do blame their circumstances. The two perspectives are mutually exclusive: that is, people may share the same circumstances, but one is left attributing their interpretation to themselves, the other attributing his or her interpretation to the circumstances they faced. We may want to think that our environments or something that happened in our past lives accounts for the way we are today. This is patently untenable. From the same conditions of life come people who are stoic and others who want to blame the world for their troubles.

Not always, of course. But blaming one's lack of responsibility on the circumstances can be a handy excuse in our time. To get a good perspective in this we can call on the playwright and social critic George Bernard Shaw:

> *"The people who get on in this world are the people who get up and look for the*

circumstances they want and if they can't
find them, make them."

Instead of complaining to anyone who will listen that "I'm a victim of my circumstances," the people who really want to "get on in this world" either find the circumstances they want or need, or, failing that, *make* the circumstances they want or need. The people who use circumstances as an excuse for their plight are not the people who get on in this world. In other words, their intention is not to "get on" in this world, but to seek sympathy (or even largesse) for circumstances beyond their control. The people who do get on in this world either find the circumstances they want, or make those circumstances. Shaw is talking about the classic case of blaming the circumstances for one's condition. So in his way of thinking, which is not popular these days, blaming the circumstances is almost always an excuse and claiming victimization is how many people deal with it. Unacceptable, he would say. They want empathy. What they need, he avers, is the gumption to get on in this world. There are legitimate victims of circumstances. But since no one knows how to discern the difference, we are asked to treat victims of what some people claim as legitimate. It could be. It could not be. Shaw is saying there is a way of discerning the real from the mere excuse: ask them what their *intentions* are in this world. Courage does not evolve from cowardice. Responsibility does not evolve from empathy or sympathy indulgence.

####

So it is clear that the pathways of our lives come from the pathways of our intentions. We might hope that it were that simple. But it isn't. That is almost the fairy tale version. The world you live in today comes from the conversations that our 7 billion or so people on earth engaged in yesterday. And from their intentions. No one's life is ever a blank slate. The real world will be an admixture of all of those conversations and what people did about them. Most intentions – although they are private – have to be carried out in the real world. That real world is full of randomness, rationality, and indifference. It is unpredictable because it is incomprehensible.

To get a sense of what the average person is up against, we might tune in on Rachel, an average worker in an average organization on an average day in her life. It is her mind we are tapping, so let's do this in third person:

> *I'm going to be late to work if I don't get some
> help with the chores around here.* It is her
> intention to get to work on time but to see to
> the children's (and probably her husband's)
> needs, and to make sure the children have
> their lunch for school, are properly dressed,
> have what they need for the day. She intended
> to look good today, but when she caught
> herself in the mirror, she thought she didn't
> like the outfit she had chosen, and she was
> having a bad hair day (not intended). *When
> the time came to leave the house, she had
> intended to check that the doors were locked,
> but she didn't have time. On the way to work,
> she tried to think about what she had to do
> and how to do the kind of triage on what she
> assumed were her duties. But, damn, her
> gauge said she was running out of gas and
> she might get stuck in a traffic jam.* Neither
> of those was anything she intended.

The traffic was not as bad as she thought it might be. On her way to work, she thought of a zillion things she had to do that had nothing to do with her work (e.g., make that doctor's appointment, take the children to the dentist after school tomorrow, have that talk with her husband he had been talking about, pick up the cleaning, stop by the market to get something for supper, call her ailing mother this evening, do something about her hair, shop for some new clothes for work, figure out a better way to organize the mornings so they were not so hectic, maybe carve out some time to practice her piano again, start talking about what the family may want to do for this year's vacation, take the car in for some routine maintenance, finish the book she had been reading, lose some weight, find some time for herself, be more available to her children with their homework and other problems, maybe get a pedicure if that would make her more attractive to her husband, write a batch of thank-you notes for what the grandparents sent the children for their birthdays, do a better job of organizing grocery-shopping, and generally to make family life more like, well, like it should be. Those were just some of her intentions. When she arrived at work (pretty much on time), someone had parked in her usual place so she had to hunt for another not too far away. She couldn't find a place in the shade so she had to park farther away in the sun. Not her intention. It was her intention to walk the stairs in order to get a little exercise, but when she glanced at her watch, she decided she didn't have enough time, so she opted for the elevator which was actually no faster. That also was not her intention. She arrived at her cubicle, having broken the heel of her shoe. She turned everything on, and found that her computer was not booting up as it should. So she had to call IT to get someone to look at it. Neither of those were actually her intention. She was talking on the phone to her boss to set up her annual performance review when Mary, her team leader stopped by to say there would be a meeting at ten and could she attend. She had intended to get caught up with some other loose ends but said she would attend. So she had to look at her notes from the last meeting, but couldn't find them. Nothing happened at the meeting that seemed in any way related to what she had intended to accomplish that morning. Her phone was ringing when she returned from the meeting. It was the doctor's office returning her call. She still had to make that appointment with her boss. At lunch, she had to listen to Mary complaining about the performance of her team. She thought that Mary was a poor leader, but her boss had appointed Mary, so she must have something going for her that Rachel couldn't see. It was not her intention to judge, but it seemed to her that her boss wasn't much of a manager either. By the time her work day was ending, Rachel looked at her to-do list. There was nothing scratched off as having been accomplished. Well, there was always tomorrow. Maybe there wouldn't be so many interruptions. The traffic on the way hone was fierce. She dreamt of a country road with no cars, lots of trees, and birds singing. That would be her intention if she were running things. She was trying hard to remember that she had to stop by the cleaners, and pick up some needed things on her list at the market. When she got home and was parking in the garage, she noticed her car's engine seemed to be overheating. By the time she fixed dinner and tidied up, she felt exhausted. She made a note to try again to reach her boss tomorrow morning. Her husband was grumpy and the children hyperactive.

Most people intend well most of the time. But the time needed for Rachel's intentions seemed never to come – what with procrastination, interruptions, and the demands that come from having her own intentions superseded by the demands of the company that provided her with a regular paycheck, her own family's needs, and the sheer complexity and speed of her days passing by. More than half of adults surveyed said that they were not satisfied with the lives they had. Rachel wondered if she was one of those, but sleep came on (not her intention) and she escaped life for yet another day.

"Busyness" is often offered as an excuse to ourselves or others for not following our own intentions. Yet that is a questionable excuse, since other people who live in the same hurry-scurry world we live in manage to pursue at least some of their long-term intentions. We know that *the pathways of our lives come from having worthy long-term intentions for our lives ahead.* But what if those personal intentions get superseded by what we take to be the imperatives of the day, and finally fade away? Then we are left to follow someone else's intentions for us, or the popular pathways of the day.

Your doctor will tell you what's good for you. Your doctor doesn't always take his or her own advice. Your financial advisor will tell you what's good for you. But your financial advisor is not you, and doesn't always follow the advice given to you. Commercial advertisers will tell you what you need, which is almost invariably what they are selling. What's going on here? It has been observed many times: *If you know the difference between good advice and bad advice, you don't need advice.* Your friends will tell you either directly or indirectly (by what they do) how to live. But that might be their pathway, and not necessarily the pathway you need to be following. It comes down to who *owns* your life, and who is responsible for it. It's unlikely that you have even one friend who would die for you – who would take your place if you were dying. Neither would your doctor. So do you want to blindly take advice from someone who has no "skin" in *your* game? Advice about how to live and what to do about your troubles increase exponentially in today's world. There is more advice than can possibly be used by any person. The supply outpaces the demand by far.

Journalist and social observer Ed Howe put a point on the dilemma:

> *"If you want to save money, don't eat anything: this advice is impractical, but so is most good advice."*

And Lord Chesterfield reminds us:

*"Advice is seldom welcome, and those who
need it the most, like it the least."*

We pay for our doctor's advice. But some people don't do what the doctor says. We pay for "the news." But we frequently don't see what the lesson is in it for us. Our favorite celebrities are forever offering us advice. But we usually don't have the money required to do much of anything about it. If it is about a new (and often proprietary) diet, we may try it. But we don't want to do anything that is outside our comfort zone. So why is it that those who need good advice the most are the least likely to seek it out? Could it be that any good advice would change who they are and thus make them more susceptible to good advice? There is something about who we are – our identity in the world – that we wear like armor against any advice that might require us to change. We have a tendency to seek confirmation from our friends and acquaintances, and not disconfirmation. We choose our friends carefully, and they theirs, so that neither of us is willing to change more than inconsequentially. When was the last time you got honest comments from a friend about faults you knew you had but wanted friends (or a lover) not to speak of them? Isn't that what the play and then the movie *Who's Afraid of Virginia Woolf* was all about? In the abstract, we might all express a preference for candidness. But in everyday life (which is the opposite of the abstract) we'll take pretense over candidness every time. We do the same with ourselves. We fantasize telling people what we really think of them and their opinions. But in real life, we are far more likely to say what others want to hear. We think that politicians have the corner on that. But we are all (small-p) politicians. To think back to what we have highlighted in this book, does this seem hypocritical to you?

####

One of the first self-help books in our world was the Dhammapada. It was about taking the right path in life. And now we know that taking the right path in life has to do with the worthiness of our intentions, and with the wisdom and the effort required to pursue and fulfill those intentions. Mark Twain once remarked:

> "When I think of the number of disagreeable people that I know who have gone to a better world, I am sure hell won't be so bad at all."

Most of the early tracts about how to live didn't have a heaven or a hell to work with. They addressed the here and now. They were about how to take the right path in this life in order to become a better person. So that's what we are talking about here. If you have worthy intentions, do your damnedest to get on and stay on the right path for your life. If they are worthy, they will be *efficacious* – that is, to the benefit of others and the larger society as well as to you. The pathway your intentions take you will benefit every person you come in contact with. They will be better people just for knowing you, for meeting you along the way.

We influence other people, and they us, all through life. When the French philosopher Cioran made the following comment, this was what he was referring to:

> "The most important choice you will ever make in life is who to have as parents."

He was using "parents" as a metaphor for all those we permit to influence us. If you are a good person (efficacious), those you permit to influence you will be efficacious people. If not, you may be influenced by the wrong people, who bring to you wrong ideas, wrong opinions, wrong perspectives, wrong paths, wrong intentions. If the people you have bartered your life for are not good for you and the larger society, they will be bad for you and the larger society. You have to know the difference. This book is intended to help you to see the difference, and to act upon it. What a different world this would be if we were capable of following Evan Esar's advice:

> *"The best time to give advice to your children is while they're still young enough to believe you know what you're talking about."*

In this sense, all the people you know are your "children." You may be their "child." Influence works both ways. Be prudent. Be intentional. Think first. And then ask the question that will propel both of you in the right direction. That's where the pathways of life come from.

11 Collective (Conglomerate) Intention

Every person who has an intention may encounter obstacles to carrying it out. Those obstacles will be either internal or external, as we have seen. That individual case is easy to understand, even though it is rarely all that easy to carry out. The internal obstacles are things like busyness and procrastination. The external obstacles are that other people and the real world have intentions of their own. They very seldom have any interest in helping us to carry out our intentions. Other people and the world in general have their own intentions (or in the case of the larger world, its teleology – its own impetus). Most of the things that happen in the world around us are wholly independent of any intention we might have. We live in a whorl of intentions, of happenings. Our personal intentions don't count for much in a world of billions of people having many billions of intentions every minute of every day. The stock market cannot be manipulated in sum by any one individual, nor can blowing or talking to the dice in a crap game.

There are a few things we can control. There are a great many things we cannot personally control. One of them is your pet cat. So on top of the complexities of personal intentions and their irrelevance to other people and the world we live in, there is another issue of vital importance to those who have intentions that involve other people. And that is the matter of *collective intention.*

####

We can look at this matter of *collective intention* from a number of intriguing perspectives:

1. There is the perspective of you watching television, a film, or reading a book or listening to music.
2. There is the perspective of you engaging in any kind of casual conversation with another person.
3. There is the perspective of you being involved in any kind of social gathering, like a "party" or some ad hoc activism.

In addition to these, there are ways of looking at the ramifications of collective intention –

4. In a friendship, partnership, or a love affair or marriage;
5. In a formal group, a team, or an organization.
6. In the changing tides and destiny of a society or a pop culture.
7. And when you are simply talking to yourself about your intentions – and, yes, that is a collective.

Those may not cover every possibility. But they may suffice for enhancing our understanding of the role of intention in life in our worlds.

You and Your Indirect Connection with Your World

You listen to your radio. If you are actually paying attention, then that is an indirect connection with the world you live in. You attend a concert or the theater or a ball game or rodeo. That is also an indirect connection with the world you inhabit. When you are watching television, a film, or reading a book, you are perhaps a passive participant in a complex collective that makes the whole process possible. The few or many people involved in bringing that kind of involvement to you have intentions. You may or may not have a specific intention for your involvement.

That may make no difference. When reading a book, you are not aware of the dozens of people who made it possible for you to be holding that book (or tablet) in your hands. The author(s) had some intention in mind. If they didn't, they would not have spent the time and made the effort to write the book, or stream it. There were probably editors and copy editors and their employers. If they didn't have some intention in doing what they did to make it possible, their employers did. Basically, their intention had little to do with you personally, or to make your life better. It is far more likely that the complex of decisions made had more to do with whether or not there was some profit to be made. If the author was a celebrity, it could have something to do with the prestige involved, rather than the money. Independent booksellers choose to stock the books they think their clientele might want to buy. Amazon, being the leading book distributor, markets the books its decision-makers think may sell online (with appropriate blurbs based on rank-order sales). In all, it is a complex collective that includes the buyer.

But the most effective source of your interest in a book is most likely to come from a friend or a colleague (or even a book club – or Oprah's – recommendation. Or maybe you heard about it in college. We use many filters in becoming aware of the existence of any book we might want to buy, or to read. If your social circles are comprised of non-readers, you are likely to get a recommendation simply because the book is reportedly popular in the *conversations* the people you know engage in. Rarely do people carry around a list of books they want to immerse themselves in before they die. Most homes today do not shelve a single book unless it is a best-seller. And that is a status symbol, not learning material.

So whether it is a book, a movie, or a television show, most people are inclined to tune in by word-of-mouth, or in order to keep up with the people they want to keep up with. So there are obviously intentions involved in the production and the consumption of the artifacts and orientations of the popular culture of the time. That pop culture doesn't exist in any tangible way (beyond the experts who explain it to us). So we absorb the pop culture inadvertently – not by intention but by osmosis – simply because we are immersed in it in all of our waking hours. The pop culture we imbibe is likely to have reached us via the people we hang out with most of the time.

It is the world we know. There may be multiple perspectives on that "same" world. But we avoid them unless we encounter them in our indirect contact (books, movies, television, etc.) with them. Some pop music becomes "our" music because the people we know "like" it and listen to it almost exclusively. We see our world through the perspective we gain from watching other people, and inadvertently by the cultural orientations that seep into us from our indirect connection with our world.

The reigning explanation in the larger culture is that of cause-and-effect: singular things happen, and they are expected to have a singular effect. In the real world, that's hardly ever the case. There are multiple effects from singular causes, and more commonly there are multiple causes for any effect. Diseases, for example, are never purely the cause of something biological or physiological. They always have concomitant psychosocial causes. And vice versa: psychosocial disorders always have concomitant (not necessarily causative) health hazards. Contagious diseases occur where most people are not immune. Contagious psychic disorders also occur where the fewest people are immune. Our "healthcare" system, driven by medicine, rarely includes these factors in their diagnoses or their thinking about etiology. The pop culture is not a culture that rewards health. It is the kind of culture based on the economies of illness and disease. This is, after all, often one of the key topics of any conversation. What we imbibe from the pop culture is more likely how to be sick than how to be well. In most novels and most television dramas, who gets the most attention?

One can't imagine that it was anyone's actual intention that our society should be as sick as it is. But the pop culture has its influence thanks to what might be called "collective intention." What people believe is not necessarily good for them, or their health. And belief is not a biological phenomenon but a psychosocial phenomenon. *Beliefs,* as with the Aztec and the Anasazi, have accounted for the demise of at least as many human civilizations as have diseases of the body. Maybe not *intended,* but every human group or civilization has its own teleology – its own destiny – which emanates from its collective, its unique beliefs.

No one intends that bad things come from what are taken as good beliefs. But they do. So the question is: What are any individual's intentions in imbibing the beliefs of the collective? That's the only immunity there is for the individual in a collective – whether two people engaged in a conversation, or millions imbibing the same beliefs, without realizing the untoward influence this may have on their lives or *their* destiny.

You and Your Direct Connection with Your World

The fundamental dynamic in any human grouping is the conversations that occur. They may seem to be as harmless as the air we breathe, because ubiquitous. But any intercourse between humans has its consequences. And the basic form of intercourse is conversation.

The interactive nature of conversation means that both parties are influenced. Eric Hoffer referred to conversation as *a kind of copulation of the minds involved*. You can't have a conversation until you have a mind.

And minds influence one another in the conversations that erupt wherever humans encounter one another at a crossroad – on a plane or at a party or in an occupational group. People seem poised to capture one another in a conversation...to follow Hoffer, this appears from a distance to be a kind of predatory copulation, even if consensual.

There are no harmless conversations. All conversations have consequences – for good or for ill. About good conversations, Ralph Waldo Emerson wrote in his piece "Social Aims":

> *"In good conversation parties don't speak to*
> *the words, but to the meanings of each other."*

One way of interpreting this is that a good conversation requires good people. Good people do not engage in alternate monologues (competing for merely verbal advantage), but in a dialogue, where what impels the conversation forward is the *meanings* they can call up of what the other may be saying.

The American humorist Josh Billings offered this perspective in his "Sollum Thoughts" (part of Billings' humor lay in the way he spelled things according to how they sounded, not the way they were supposed to be spelled):

> *"Conversashun should be enlivened with wit,*
> *not compozed ov it."*

The issue here is not what is said, but the meaning and the consequences of what is said. It is not a verbal sparring match. What is meant is more important than what is said. And if what is meant is efficacious (good for both parties and for the larger collective, like the community) that would be what Emerson refers to as a "good" conversation. There are ways in which two minds copulating produce good results for both, and thus for their larger collective.

Most conversations don't go anywhere. They seem to be intended just to produce good (or bad) feelings in the participants, and to give them an opportunity to exercise their jaws by telling the other person what they know. When they were young children, their conversation often ended in a question. As they got older, they ceased wondering (asking questions) and fell into the telling mode. They tell the other person what they happen to know (reciprocally) in order to bond because they now know some of the same things the other person knows.

An argument is quite different. In an argument, they don't want to share. They want to prove their correctness and discredit the other person's facts or opinions. A trial by jury is an argument. Marital discord leads to arguments. Negotiating is an argument in disguise: it's an argument to determine who gets the best deal. Older children are known for falling into arguments with their parents or elders. That's just bad parenting.

In his *Maxims* (1665), La Rochefoucauld wrote:

> *"One of the reasons why so few people are to be found who seem sensible and pleasant in conversation is that almost everybody is thinking about what he wants to say himself rather than answering clearly what is being said to him."*

Add to that an observation by Kim Hubbard (in his *Hoss Sense and Nonsense*):

> *"Th' only way t' entertain some folks is t' listen t' em."*

And there you have the remarkable difference between a dialogue and alternate monologues. In a dialogue, the parties are committed (and capable) of responding to what the other says, and of going together where the dialogue leads them. Since most people want to talk about themselves, the conversation is really an instance of alternate monologues. You talk and then I talk, but rarely about the same thing.

What Hubbard was trying to get across is that people are accustomed to being "entertained," and that the most expedient way of entertaining them is to listen to them talk about themselves. (One finds the same sentiment in Carnegie's *How to Win Friends and Influence People*. If you want people to "like" you, ask them to talk about themselves. Those who are always talking about themselves don't have many friends...except perhaps in the social media, where our "friends" expect us to befriend them.)

If the other party in a conversation is thinking not about what the other person said, but about what he or she is going to say next, as Rochefoucauld observed, it is once again not a dialogue but a series of alternate monologues.

There are two other perspectives on this subject that may need to be raised. **One** is that the reason why most conversations turn out to be a waste of time for one or both is that they did not agree (even implicitly) about what their conversation was supposed to accomplish. They may each have felt good about their conversation. But they shared no *collective intention* about what was to be accomplished. That's why such conversations wander all over the place. They have no mutual end in mind – what John Gardner referred to as "common cause." They had no mutual ends in mind for their conversation. They are not on the same path to roughly the same place.

Two: Such casual conversations may be an example of the blind leading the blind. Conversations may not be intended to produce anything of value. The people are just "talking." But it makes a great deal of difference who those people are. There is a Chinese saying:

"A single conversation across the table with a wise man is better than ten years' study of books."

A single conversation is worth more than many years studying books? Why? Because wisdom is rare, talk is cheap. If your conversations are always with people who are wiser than you are, you will gain by listening. Perhaps the reason people don't listen is that their experience is that the other person is no smarter than they are. But how would an unwise person identify someone smarter than they are? It is a characteristic of "average" people that they cannot discriminate the wise from the unwise. And even if they could, they would not want to listen when they could be talking – a common prejudice of most people. Why, when they have to expend the same level of effort to remain ignorant as would be required to be much wiser than "average" or normative?

And recall that all conversations have consequences … for you and thus for the destiny of all parties involved. Those consequences will vary with what you bring to the conversation. If it is not your intention to make your conversations efficacious – that is, of real benefit to both, and to the larger collective – they probably will not be. At the very least, your conversations set the pathways of your life. They are that important.

About Collectives and "Their" Intentions

If you go to a party where you know everyone, your conversations will be different than they would be if you didn't know the people at the party. If you are seated at the football game with the fans of your team, you will try hard to perform as the other fans perform. It is most likely you will not conform to the fans of the opposing team. If you are demonstrating for some cause or other, you will recognize the regulars, who seem to know what to do and when. They may be paid demonstrators, in which case you will follow their lead. You might think that an ad hoc demonstration would be chaotic. And it can be. But after you have attended the practice, you will notice that the collection of people seem to be functioning on the basis of a common intention, just as they might at a wedding, which is usually rehearsed. Social gatherings will vary from those that seem to have protocols that are imperative, to a rag-tag bunch of people each doing his or her own thing. That is, some will seem to be collecting around a centralizing intention, and others will not.

As Aldous Huxley wrote in *Ends and Means:*

> *"To be a member of a crowd is an experience closely akin to alcoholic intoxication. Most human beings feel a craving to escape from the cramping limitations of their ego, to take periodical holidays from their all too familiar, all too squalid little selves."*

If this reminds you of some social gatherings you have attended, that may have been what was intended. If you're merely observing a march for some cause, you could hardly avoid thinking that the marchers were so exuberant because they were escaping from something. If what they are escaping is the likely banality of their everyday lives, it is as if they had been released from captivity. Have you never attended a party where that seemed to be the case? Huxley may be heavy-handed here. But don't you have the feeling that he is onto something fundamental about human nature? Have you ever attended Mardi Gras in New Orleans, or caught snippets of it on television? Have you ever observed Irish or African celebrations? Were the people celebrating the cause of the celebration? Or were they celebrating their momentary escape from their all too familiar lives, as in *Dancing at Lughnasa* or *Mama Mia*? The Irish "wake" has an implicit intention, which is what?

Gustav Le Bon, in his seminal study entitled *The Crowd* (1895) offered his perspective as follows:

> *"In a crowd every sentiment and act is contagious, and contagious to such a degree that an individual readily sacrifices his personal interest to the collective interest."*

It is the collective interest of the crowd that constitutes what amounts to an intention. It does not emanate from one person, but from the crowd itself. The crowd, as police everywhere in the world have learned, has no conscience. It is like a conflagration about to erupt in ways no one could predict. It is controlled by the contagion Le Bon writes about, but is at any moment capable of going out of control and undertaking acts of violence and brutality that no *individual* in the crowd would ever commit.

Perhaps this is what Huxley meant by his comment about alcoholic intoxication. At a free-wheeling party, fueled indeed by alcohol, people will say and do things they would not ordinarily say or do. Their intention is not to embarrass themselves, but to go out of control, and be controlled by the ethos of the gathering. We can't say that such social gatherings have an "intention." But there is a sense in which they do. And the people who gather are willing to sacrifice their personal interests to the interest of the collective. That is something that rarely happens in other kinds of social enterprises, as we will see.

The Difficulties of Creating *Collective* Intention

Aristotle wanted us to think of a friend as a *second self.* This, he thought, was what made friendship ethical as opposed to exploitative. People who claim to be friends may be so only because they mutually exploit one another. They take what they need from the relationship, and permit the other to take from it what he or she needs. People expect friends to salve their loneliness, for example.

Ambrose Bierce, in his satirical compendium *The Devil's Dictionary,* came at the friendship thing from the opposite point of view by defining a friendless person by the following adjective:

> *"Friendless, adj. Having no favors to bestow.*
> *Destitute of fortune. Addicted to utterance of*
> *truth and common sense."*

He is saying indirectly that people who have favors to bestow are likely to have lots of "friends." He is also saying that people who have fortunes to distribute are also likely to have lots of "friends." And, perhaps most importantly, he is saying that people who are addicted to telling the truth and who can be depended upon to relate to others as common sense might dictate are people who will be relatively *friendless.* The intentions of people in a friendship are likely to be self-serving but secretive. Their motives are likely to be other than they are purported to be – in other words, that friendship seems often to be a relationship between two hypocrites (recall our earlier exploration of hypocrisy, so rampant in this world of ours).

Partnerships often suffer the same difficulties. When one or more people use partnerships for their own personal advantage, there will be troubles ahead. The same could be said for love affairs. If they are consummated for their own personal interests – whatever the cost to the other person – they will brew all kinds of problems from which one or both will suffer. Perhaps nowhere will you see this portrayed with all of its endless nuances than in the film, (English title) *Dangerous Liaisons* – unless of course you are privy to an equally sordid affair (by gossip) in your own community. Another microscopic look at the intricate consequences of such liaisons is the film, *Damage*. The first looks at a love affair as a game of seduction. And playing this game is very simple. Just lie, cheat, deceive, betray – anything goes in the game to win the prize. The plot of *Damage* is all about two lovers, a middle-aged man and his son's fiancé. To pay any price for their passion leads to the "damage" for all of those around the obsessed lovers. All of the characters in these two stories had intentions of their own. But the consequences of their actions were not what they intended. *There is intention – the process – and there are its consequences, which can be quite unintended.* So are people responsible for only the process, or does their responsibility include the unintended consequences? In his "Study" of three great minds, *An Experiment in Depth*, P. W. Martin wrote:

> *"What passes as love between man and woman can be many things. Promiscuity, possessiveness, misuse of sex for purposes of power, are all highly disintegrative...."*

You could undoubtedly add a couple dozen more hidden agendas to that list. What people label as love depends upon each individual's perspective on such relationships. But the important point is that they are all highly *disintegrative*. That means they damage the relationship and are a kind of poison to those who are affected by the unintended consequences and to the social collective to which those people belong.

Of course there are normative love affairs – that is, those that are endorsed by the pop culture. There are even efficacious love affairs.

But those don't capture our attention as consumers, and therefore do not capture the attention of writers, script-writers, or producers of our entertainments. We want to read about or watch those that have bad unintended consequences. We are attracted by the dramatic, not by the humdrum of our everyday lives. We may intend the best, but we are more interested in the worst.

The perspective that may be most enlightening is that of marriage. And what we see there is this: if the two people involved are there for their own selfish motives, there will be troubles. It is only when they both attune themselves to making the *marriage* an ideal one – when that is their collective intention – that the relationship will produce what they want from it. That is, if they see themselves as stewards of the dreamed-about institution, they will have a good relationship. If they see it only from their self-serving point of view, they will not.

Collective intention means that the people involved share the same intention for their marriage. Obviously this is not an imperative of most marriages, and this is the most important reason why people do not "live happily ever after." They may make some compromises in order to stay together. But a good marriage cannot be made out of unworthy individual intentions. What is an "unworthy" individual intention? It is one that is pursued unilaterally. And it is unworthy because it is not beneficial to the larger social collective to which they belong.

This difficulty is even more obvious when you focus upon some of the more formal organizations involving people. A religion is intended to bring people together under the rubric of a collective intention. But the individuals who make up the congregation argue and fuss with one another sometimes as if they didn't belong to the same group.

My Irish (immigrant) grandfather was one of the last self-sufficient farmers. He and my grandmother took care of everything that needed taking care of, from milking by hand 15 cows morning and night, 24/7. If something wasn't working, it was up to them to fix it. They put away food and feed for the winter months. My grandfather had a "cash" crop, which he sold in order to have some dollars. He bought horses, trained them to work in teams of two or four, and sold them as teams. As he once told me when I was really too young to really understand (around age 4): "Son," he said to this wide-eyed kid, "when you have four horses under harness and they work as a team, you have about six horsepower. But if they are not trained to work as a team, you have less than two horsepower. When they pull together (*collective intention?*), you can get twice as much work done in half the time." That's why other farmers were eager to buy his teams.

Let's look at a basketball or football team. If they work as a team, it's as if they had one or two more players in the game than did their opponents. If there is an 8-person "team" in a larger organization (so-called just because it a cliché to do so) and they function as if by a collective intention, they may be able to accomplish twice as much in half the time. But it doesn't work that way with 8 *individuals,* who may be merely *referred* to as a "team." Because they have different agendas, and are not functioning by collective intention, it will likely take them at least twice as long to accomplish half as much.

Collective intention is critical in formal organizations. Their "leaders" are continuously looking for the "magic bullet" that puts everyone "on the same page" (to use an overused cliché of the day). The top person may have intentions for the performance of his or her organization. But when any executive's intention has to be carried out by a mishmash of other people, things usually don't turn out as intended. Those other people were not brought up – nor were they trained – to work in concert with other people. They were brought up as individuals. They are likely to remain individualistic until they die – in spite of the entreaties of their bosses. So most formal organizations pay twice as much for half the accomplishments intended. All for want of *collective* intention. The bosses try every trick that comes along in the pop-culture. There is an ancient Chinese saying that doing the same thing over and over again with no better results is a form of insanity. Indeed it may be. It would not be the only form of insanity one can observe in formal organizations. They face the same set of difficulties as in marriages: What is this marriage *for?* Why does IT exist? If worthy, how can IT be nurtured? IT requires collective intention. For larger organizations: What is the rationale for ITS existence? What is it *for?* How does this organization bear upon the society's destiny? If it doesn't make the people who work there better *people,* it has failed. If it has teams within, the same kinds of questions apply. How do you put people on the same worthy path? If a team meeting (for example) doesn't make better people out of its members, the meeting has failed its goals. If a marriage does not make better people out of the two spouses, it has failed its goals.

The marriage counselor is likely to talk to the people involved as individuals, leaving the third party (the marriage itself) to sicken and die. The higher the quality of the marriage (or any organization), the more efficacious it will be for the people who live in it, and for it. How many people are required to take a course in marriage-making *before* they get involved? How many people in an organization were required to take a course in organization-making *before* they got involved?

It is the case that the organization (or the marriage) will be no better than the people who make it go, at every level. But it is also the case that the people who make it function can generally be no better than the organization they work for. This may seem circular because it is. If the larger collective is not healthy and humanizing, the people involved cannot be healthy or growing as human beings. Collective intention begins with the story of the collective. If the persons who have a role to play in *its* story but fail to do so competently, the story intended will wither and die in those persons' own lifetimes. You can pay people well for being a part of a team or an organization, but this alone does not make them competent to fulfill a role therein. People may get what they want out of a marriage. But if they don't make the marriage capable of providing what they want, then it is very likely they won't get what they want out of that marriage. If we don't make of our society what it ought to be, "it" cannot provide its constituents what they want and need.

To create a great marriage or a great society, there has to be a *collective intention* to do so. Just like the players on the stage, if they don't have a collective intention to make the theater (or *our* theater, as Shakespeare said) – if *we* don't have the collective intention and the wherewithal to make our collective performance successful, the theater of our lives will not be successful.

How do you confer a benefit on an unwilling person? From the time of the ancient Greeks, we have known you can't. But, whether voluntary or involuntary, if it is *necessary*, it will likely happen. If it is not *necessary*, the benefit will not see the light of day. A good marriage produces good people. A good society produces good people. First we make our institutions and then they make us.

The Rev. E. J. Hardy entitled his 1910 book, *How to Be Happy Though Married*. In more contemporary times, we may need a book entitled *How to Be Happy Though Employed by a Modern Organization.*

12 The Omnipresent Collective: the Pop Culture

Wherever you go, there *you* are. And wherever you go, the popular culture will be your environment. The pop culture is the baggage you take with you wherever you go. It is therefore omnipresent: It is there wherever you go. It is the scabbard for your mind. It is like the air you breathe. It influences you whether you are aware of it or not. You were born into it because it is omnipresent, and the people who took you home were representatives of the pop culture. It was done the way they do it not because that was the best way, but simply because that was the way it was done in that pop culture. You will be handled the way you are handled because that was the currently-popular way of doing so. You will be swaddled or clothed as you are because that was the currently-popular way of doing so. You will be talked to, treated, and fed the way you were because that was then the currently-popular way of doing so. If you were born into a cannibal culture, you wouldn't see anything wrong with it. And if "everybody" your parents knew were doing those popular things in the popular ways – even tripping to Disney World, it is likely you've been there and may have the photos to prove it.

All cultures have protocols for doing what is being done, and taboos against doing what should not be done. For example, you are not supposed to talk about your bowel troubles or your sexual peccadilloes at a festive dinner party. But you are not likely to have been at a festive dinner party if such were not *de rigueur* in your social class or social circles. You were once expected to be witty. Now you may be expected not to be so witty that you make others feel inferior. Or that you make yourself feel superior. That different classes have different perspectives about most things is well portrayed in the film, *Beatriz at Dinner*. You will know what "class" you belong to because the world you live in will be reminding you at all times. But that is what Edith Wharton and Jane Austen and many other novelists we know wrote about, isn't it? As James Baldwin put it:

> *"If the world tells you how you are going to be treated, you are in trouble."*

And if you try to cross the line between how you are seen and the way you would like to be seen (*Beatriz* again), you are asking for trouble. We Americans may be accused of being "racist," but our more pervasive prejudice is that we are anti-intellectual: As a people, we don't like to think, and we inherently dislike anyone who tries to make us think. Don Marquis asked us to think about this when he quipped:

> *"If you make people think they're thinking, they'll love you; but if you really make them think, they'll hate you."*

We would rather be complacent in our lifestyles than be challenged. We like our comfort zones. No matter how much we might complain about our lives, don't try to change us. We don't understand even half of what we pretend to understand. That is why we prefer others like us – who are good at performing in public – no matter how shallow or unjustified that performance may actually be.

If you are poorly parked, someone may tell you. If you are stupid, not even your best friends may tell you.

The pop culture (which happens to be the one Americans prefer) is the ultimate source of what we know, of how we feel, of what we pay attention to and how we express ourselves. It has little to say about our private lives, except if it makes you feel good, do it. But about our public lives, it has long lists of do's and don't. Don't read, for example. "No one" reads any more. If you don't, you'll fit in. But if you do, just don't let it show by talking about it, for it may be offensive to someone who is into political correctness. The pop culture is ubiquitous, pervasive, and inescapable. It is full of prescriptions and proscriptions about performing in everyday life (as Goffman famously wrote in his book *The Presentation of Self in Everyday Life*). If you don't know what those prescriptions and proscriptions are, just do what everyone else does. If you're in the midst of partisan fans, just do what they do. If they gyrate, then learn how to gyrate. If they are duplicitous, learn how to be duplicitous, and so on and on. We don't go to school to learn about our pop culture and how it influences us. Because we are immersed in it during all of our waking hours, we rarely ever acknowledge it. It is simply the largest part of who we are – and of how we think about things. Our minds, before all else, refract the pop culture. And in some incomprehensible way, the pop culture refracts our collective minds.

Let's go to example. Suppose you needed to go to the grocery store to get some groceries. What you will find there is what sells – that is, what the popular items are that the people who go there buy. You may not find what *you* went there for. You will find what is popular with the people who shop there. Whether a small corner store or an elaborate supermarket, all you can find there most prominently displayed will be the items that the people who shop there, buy there.

Or you might go clothes or shoe shopping. It's likely you won't find what you want, so your expedition is mainly to find out what you want from what's in the stores (or online). They are not there for *you*. They are there for what's in fashion and thus what people are buying. You won't find the sweater there or the shoes there that you bought two years ago.

Those are now out of fashion, having been displaced by the newest fashions.

Or you might go car shopping. The first thing you will notice is that the current models look pretty much the same, regardless of brand. The second thing you will notice may be that they are distinguishable, but only technologically. Then you might notice that cars in general have gotten a lot more costly. That's mainly because of the technology: the more gadgets, the more cost. And then there are the technics of manufacturing. Metal and plastic forming are not what they used to be. Nor is the assembly. Cars are simply more complicated than they used to be. Such technologies have increased the cost to about twice what it was at the end of the last century. The only thing that has really been constant is depreciation: guaranteed. Because the look and the technologies behind the dash drive up the cost, but do not drive down the cost. There are more colors and fancy wheels to choose from.

For money, you can access the programs on television you used to be addicted to. Or, you can simply get addicted to what's available. The pop culture, presumably as a result of what people want, is formidably present. But when was it possible to have a plot line that didn't involve the latest communication technologies? Even Archie Bunker (of *All In the Family)* had the kind of telephone that was in fashion at that time. College students today may not be heavy television users. But who hasn't observed them leaving their dorm mates behind as they ambled off to their first (usually 10 o'clock) classes, and in the lobby outside the assigned classroom, call their dorm mates (via "smart" phone) that they had left 15 minutes ago in order to "stay connected." To signify to others that they are students, they all have competitive backpacks – with no more than a few books but with the requisite computer and other electronic gadgetry.

If you go to get a haircut, it will be the kind of haircut that is in fashion, not the one you wanted. Why do sorority girls look so much alike? They look alike because they are selected for how they look, and they use the same cosmetics. It is the same for the boys. There are haircuts and tight jeans that are "in" (most popular) and haircuts and tailored pants that are "out" (of fashion). If you went looking for stuff that would make you look like you were "in," that's what you would find.

The most consequential fashions in any culture or subculture are the way you think about things, how you comport yourself, and the way you express your feelings and opinions. We are not normally aware that the way we think, the way we feel, and what we do (and how we do it) are derived mainly from the pop culture. We are inclined to think that our thoughts are *our* thoughts, that our feelings are *our* feelings, that what we like, what we don't like, and how we express ourselves are artifacts of our unique selves. All you need, to see how pervasive the pop culture is in our lives, is to listen to people talk. The cliché "you know" is sprinkled throughout most people's talk like seasoning on a piece of meat. Ways of thinking, feeling, and doing seep into our minds with no particular intention on our part. We are not aware of this happening, because it is so pervasive, so insidious as our visual and auditory environment, that we don't notice it. We think like others in our pop culture environment think. We share our interpretations of our external and internal environments. Whenever two minds encounter one another, as we have seen, and to cite Eric Hoffer once again (for good reason):

> *"There are no chaste minds. Minds copulate wherever they meet."*

This is a very useful perspective. What it may mean is that we are influenced by those we imagine we are influencing. Whenever minds meet in a conversation, say, they copulate. This suggests that there will be consequences for one or both, but that there is no way of actually determining what those consequences will be. We know that such encounters are asymmetrical. That is, that one of the two people's intentions will affect the outcome more than the other person's. Or, one person may have the power to specify the consequences – as in Marine boot camp. Or, your senior professor may have the power to approve your graduation, or not. It's likely that people who lived in the 19th-century wouldn't understand a film about modern marriage. The kind of symmetry (or "equality," if you will) portrayed there didn't exist in the 19th-century. People had their superior or inferior roles to play. They simply played their given roles as well as they were capable. Something other than their given roles was simply not for conversation, or bickering. Then along came "women's liberation," coffee klatches, and conversations about the unthinkable – a "liberated" woman. It started as an idea in a conversation and became a social movement.

Or, it could mean that there are no independent minds. All minds are created and maintained in a social context. Ideas – and particularly the *meaning* of the things to be talked about – have to come from somewhere. You did not invent the ideas or the rubrics or the paradigms you impose on the world in order to understand it. Understanding is a social process, not a biological one. Bees and fleas "understand" the world they live in. But they don't talk about it like people do. We don't even see any evidence that *they* want to study us. Gnats are hardwired to do what gnats do. We are not. We are all products of some culture. And in a world like ours, with the freedom to think whatever we want to, to believe whatever we want to believe, and to do whatever we can afford to do, we must have a common source to draw from. And that common source is our pop culture. We are who we are because our pop culture is what it is. The succeeding generations are not *sui generis*. They start with the world they inherited from us (and we inherited from our predecessors) and set about to change it to enable other (they would say, superior) ways of being and doing.

All of our joys in life, and all of its trials and tribulations, come from the pop culture – modified by how we talk about such things in the *lingua franca* of our current pop culture. We evolve, we change, but not necessarily in an *efficacious* direction. When you get right down to it, the pop culture that sources us doesn't care whether we live or die. We're doing our thing, and "it" is doing its conglomerate thing in ways we cannot comprehend. Our logic might be useful to us. But its logic is nothing that any one of us controls or groups of us ever controls. We create our culture, and then our culture creates us (to paraphrase Winston Churchill about our buildings – themselves the artifacts of our pop culture).

Not unrelated, but Eric Hoffer comments elsewhere:

> *"When people are free to do as they please, they usually imitate each other."*

We know how powerful imitation (or non-biological contagion) is early on in learning how to become a human. Toddlers even learn language and internalize communication skills by imitation. They learn to say "Mommy, I love you" before they could have any cognitive understanding of what that means. We become human by imitating the humans around us. The imitation leads to all kinds of paradigmatic thinking, being, and doing. We don't learn how we are supposed to be and then do it. We imitate the others around us, and gradually become more or less like them. Dancers imitate dancers, cooks imitate cooks, and crazy people imitate crazy people.

We couldn't become humans without having humans to imitate, in much the same way as geese may "imprint" on the humans who tend them from birth. It is the pop culture at work, as the acculturated folk bring up the new and innocent folk. It happens anyway. Where humans are concerned, it's just a matter of recognizing the pop culture of the day as the major player in the story of becoming who we are. In a letter to his son in 1750, Lord Chesterfield wrote:

> *"We are, in truth, more than half what we are by imitation. The great point is, to choose good models and to study them with care."*

Advice like this is certainly well-intended. But it may be too abstract, and therefore not possible. How is a person who becomes a person by imitating others to discern a good model from a bad one? Wouldn't a person have to be committed to a worthy purpose in life to claim any unique achievement as a human being? And wouldn't that purpose have to be pursued by one's own wits and not by imitation, often by *inventing* a path rather than taking the path most taken? Lord Chesterfield, as astute as he was, may be saying that we need to find the best models we could find of being a human being, and using that as a springboard, surpassing them?

One of the problems in assessing the value of a "good model" is affinity. Quintilian (early 1st-century A.D.) captured that obstacle well:

> *"How much more readily we imitate those whom we like can scarcely be expressed."*

We like certain people and don't like certain others. We like certain of our public celebrities and don't like certain others. We like certain books and movies and don't like certain others. At work or school, we like certain of our bosses, teachers, and peers, and don't like certain others. What Quintilian is saying is that we much more readily imitate those whom we like, and do so much more frequently (and unconsciously), than those we don't particularly like. Still, there are certain things about people we like and certain things about them we don't like. We are far more likely to imitate those traits we like, even if they are criminals or aliens. Our tastes (positive or negative) channel our imitations. How the pop culture fits into this is that those people/celebrities we like may be deeply representative of the pop culture. Thus you are hooked into it indirectly.

####

If you want to get an even keener sense of how insidious and potentially pervasive the images and formulas for everyday living from the pop culture can be, consider these:

- If you see an attractive young woman somewhere, she will likely have long flowing hair these days. If she has short hair, you have to wonder if maybe she's older than she looks.

- If you see an attractive young man in exercise attire (dressed according to the pop culture prescriptions), he will likely have hairy underarms. If he doesn't, you have to wonder...?

- If you see an attractive young woman in shorts or short skirt, she is likely to have no hair on her legs. If she does, you may have to wonder...? She will also have no underarm hair. If she does, you will wonder...?

- If you see a reasonably attractive young man who has no underarm hair, you may have to wonder...?

- If you see a guy with face hair, you may think nothing of it. If you were to see a girl with face hair, or with unshaped eyebrows, you may have to wonder...?

Because of the influence of the pop culture, certain ways of appearing in public will seem "natural." Certain other ways of presenting oneself in public may seem unnatural. This is the influence of the pop culture at work. Some native people who have had no contact with the modern world will be reluctant to board an airplane. They may also believe it to be taboo to have their picture taken because that sprits their soul away from them. We moderns would consider that laughable. Some natives go naturally topless or with their penis extenders on in public. It may feel natural to them, but we moderns would be reluctant. We believe that breastfeeding in public is taboo. They may not. The pop culture is a powerful storehouse for what is permissible and what is not. It is omnipresent and omnipotent. We forget that what we believe to be reality is only one way of seeing it and dealing with it. It is ultimately what the collective – the pop culture – says it is. Those who do not see the world as you do are ignorant heathens. In taking over the world in colonial times, those humans were given a choice: see the world and its god as we do, or die. That's one way to bring them into the fold. Another way is to claim them as your children, and bring them up to see the world and behave in it as they "should" – which of course is a pop culture imperative. It changes with the pop culture of every successive generation. They will not see sex, for example, the way their grandmothers did. Nor like the same music nor have the same attitude toward work or chores. They will not harbor the same *intentions* or the same perspectives toward life as their progenitors did.

That's because their minds *may* be influenced, but not cloned. Beginning from adulthood, we evolve or devolve cognitively, not biologically. It is the pop culture that carries the collective wisdom (?) of the immediate past and the present clutch of people. It is what they make popular or fashionable in ways of thinking, of being, and of doing. The collective that rules our lives comes indirectly in a myriad of ways. For three more examples:

- If you see a male with long hair, you assume he is a musician or a professional athlete. (Or is, perhaps, in rare cases, having a problem with his gender.) Otherwise, you have to wonder...?
- The people who work at your organization, and the people who perform being executives at your organization, take great care in the way they comport themselves and in their dress and talk, in order to distinguish themselves from those other classes of people who get their paychecks there.
- On a college campus, it is fairly easy to distinguish the professors from the students. 1. The students are the ones with the backpacks. 2. Both groups have their own vernacular. Sometimes it isn't easy to translate the professors' language into the students' language. 3. What they try to share, without either one learning anything, is the pop culture of the time – like "political correctness." 4. They do not eat the same foods or shop for clothing at the same places.

The pop culture is curated by the people presently alive who use it for their own purposes. It is thus a collective resource, and a very changeable one in our world of "free" speech (as long as it meets the standards), free thinking (opining), and free love (and hate). We believe what we believe as long as those beliefs are corroborated by the groups we look to as "reference groups" (i.e., the subcultures that more directly influence the way we think, the way we feel, and the way we express ourselves). "Our Gang," so to speak: those we hang out with or look up to for leadership about how to be and how to do.

Every choice we make is an intention in disguise. Every choice made for us is an "intention" (of the pop culture) in disguise. The "disguise" comes from the fact that we think that *we* are making the choice, when all the time it is being made for us, or is at least channeling our choices. Here's a quip from the aphorist Evan Esar that may set one's thinking off on a useful path:

> *"A man picks a wife about the same way an*
> *apple picks a farmer."*

Does the apple pick the farmer? The future spouse has to choose a wife from those that may be available in his immediate environment. Indeed, she plays a key role in the whole process: she may even be disinterested because she has a better choice on the line. Why any two people fall for each other and for the consequences has a lot to do with serendipity – it depends on whether or not they have that kind of intention, and then upon some sort of magical mutual attraction. It is far from being a rational process. Notice that you cannot think through the conundrum posed above rationally. It's a metaphor. It cannot mean anything more or less than it means *to you*. Does the rain fall where you are rather than two miles away? Does that have anything to do with *your intentions*? Do we marry the person we should have married? One observer referred to this as marrying the right wrong person. As likely as not, you will marry a wrong person. But if it's the "right" wrong person, you could have a fine and lasting marriage.

The "father" of American psychology, William James, made a comment that addresses obliquely the illusion of choice:

> *"When you have to make a choice and don't make it, that in itself is a choice."*

In other words (and back to an earlier springboard), if you have an *intention* to do something or to refrain from doing that something by not trying to implement it, that is a choice – probably because other intentions arise that take precedence. You get distracted. You get diverted. The illusion of choice may (because of our peculiar pop culture thinking) lead us to believe that we're the one who is making the choice when in reality what we are choosing has already been chosen for us by forces over which we have no control. In our inescapable hubris (again, because of our pop culture and subcultures), we want to pretend that we are the agents of choice. We may fantasize that we are. But in the real world, any action or inaction on our part has multiple causatives. Most of which we are not even aware. Why did that particular apple end up in the particular farmer's hand? Why do any two particular people fall in love, or get married? Ultimately, we don't know. We could explain such things to our own or others' satisfaction. But explanations are not part of the real world: they are simply part of our cognitive worlds. It is not our choice where or when the rain falls. Nor is it our choice where or when our intentions are going to become a part of the real world.

Two quotations by Oscar Wilde here will help us to move onto a better understanding. His view was that everything that is popular is wrong. So perhaps what is unpopular could be right?

First quotation:

> *"The world has grown suspicious of anything that looks like a happily married life."*

Here he is saying that most of the troubles people have in their married life comes from the pop culture. It may not be anyone's *intention* that their married lives should be so trouble-prone. But these are the stories that get told. And therefore they are the prescriptions we have. If you are married, never talk to married people who are bickering or fighting, altogether on another path than they intended when they got married in order to "live happily ever after." That's a pop culture platitude that leads millions down the wrong path. A pop culture may be a necessary thing. But that does not necessarily make it a right thing for anyone. Why would we be suspicious of anything that looks like a happily married life? Because the stories we consume are not about that. For a gossip or a novelist to tell us a story that will keep us awake, it has to have lurid details, it has to have drama, suspense. Happy marriages don't have that. The tale hangs upon what went wrong, not what went right.

Second quotation:

> *"A person should either be a work of art, or wear a work of art."*

It is actually a work of art that gives lie to the pop culture one adheres to. A person is either mostly a conformist or mostly a nonconformist. The only immunity there is to being one of the millions of clichés of the pop culture is to consciously avoid being so. A work of art is creative. To live life creatively, Wilde may be saying, is to have a better life. The worst life is to be a shill of the pop culture and the pop subcultures one might belong to. Belonging makes you a puppet of the pop culture. You may not agree. Our aim here is not agreement or disagreement, but insight into the process of how lives get made in our modern world. The effort that Wilde had to make to be different (to BE a work of art) may be more than you would want to commit yourself to. But you may come away thinking that Wilde had an intriguing perspective on life – and thus on *intention*, still the focus of our exploration.

People make choices and decisions all day long. Thus they do have *intentions*. They may have a "planner," or they may have gotten up with intentions for the day, the planner probably not reflecting many of *their* personal intentions. The world of work often has diversions, but so does our leisure time. The demands of work take precedence over our personal intentions. We are supposed to defer those to our own time. But the demands of life away from work cause most people to defer yet again their own intentions. What are the criteria you use to do triage on what needs to be done, as contrasted with what you intended to do? The world is a busy place (so it seems), with things that interfere with our intentions. Young people still have hopes and aims for their future. Only for the tiniest minority do they ever come about.

What we learn is not how to lead ourselves, but how to procrastinate – how to put our intentions on the back burner. It may be that the few people who *do* fulfill their intentions in the modern world are people who refuse to procrastinate or to compromise their intentions. To the rest of us, they look like renegades. They look like people who don't know what's important – like picking up the laundry detergent or just having "fun."
The pop culture has room for both kinds of people. It's just that those who follow their own path seem immune to the most pervasive influences of the pop culture. That's possible of course.

Parents may try. But young children are not taught how to be immune to those influences. They are permitted (even encouraged) to watch commercial television. But commercial television is not free. The price to be paid is taking in the commercials that occur before the "filler" or the content between adverts. The real business of television is predatory – appealing to an audience in such a way that any program has the largest audience. The larger the audience, comparatively, the more that can be charged for advertising time. Commercial advertising is often more seductive than the programs they support. They have better actors (often highly-paid actors or celebrities), better graphics and color, and better writers than do the programs themselves. The people who make commercials competitively are paid more. The best often gravitate in the direction of better pay.

The purpose of the commercials is predatory. Their aim is to make business (money) for their clients. They are not there for you. They are there to win you over. If you know a 3-or 4 year-old child who does not know this, his or her parents may have failed. They may have failed because they didn't know this either, or how cleverly under-handed it can be. Or perhaps they simply don't think it is that important. If it is part of the child's entertainment, it is harmless and occupies the kids for a while. What's wrong with that? It is, after all, the pop culture at work. Everybody else is tuned in.

It is also habits or routines at work. And nothing diverts one's attention from one's intentions like habits or everyday routines can. Children can even learn how to procrastinate – how to put off doing their homework until after they have seen their shows, when most often there is no longer time to do their homework. One's long-term intentions fade from view when there is more entertaining stuff to watch. Today, part of the entertainment may come under the bed covers via their "smart" phones late at night.

It's easy to see how most people's longer-term intentions for their lives wither and die. TV requires only short-term attention. So does texting.
The intentions one may have had for one's life have been eroded and are no longer of any consequence in our world once one reaches adulthood. There has been too much codddling and too little discipline for those longer-term intentions to be important. If you ask a child what he or she wants to be when they grow up, they may respond by saying their favorite character on their favorite television show. Their parents fail them, their teachers fail them, the virtual world fails them. They have consumed lots of entertainment, but it has not put them on the right path.

As we saw at the beginning of this chapter, a person's worthy intentions (fulfilled) predict to who that person will become. Similarly, what a person has paid attention to over his or her lifetime to date will fairly well predict to the kind of life that person will be channeled to have all the rest of the tomorrows of his or her life.

To have a worthy life requires having worthy intentions and carrying them out. Otherwise you will have the kind of life available to you in the pop culture (and pop subcultures) you belong to. Your intentions with respect to your life leave you with two choices only: either decide what you would be, and then do what is necessary (as Epictetus proposed), or someone or something else (usually the pop culture) will do this for you.
No one else can "empower" you. You empower yourself by choosing worthy intentions, and then acting on them. What's worthy can range all the way from where you intend to live...and how...to doing what you can on an everyday basis to make this the world you would want to live in.

One of the best lessons I have ever seen about procrastination comes from Marcus Aurelius, to wit:

> *"Near at hand is forgetting all;*
> *near, too, all forgetting you."*

And this phrase from William James may be useful to chew on:

> *"...if one has not taken advantage of every*
> *concrete opportunity to act, one's character*
> *may remain entirely unaffected for the better."*

13 Living as Intended

It is one thing to "have" worthy intentions. It is quite another thing to be "had by" your worthy intentions. Being *had by* your worthy intentions means that you believe you have no option but to fulfill them. If you don't carry out your worthy intentions, then you have them just for your private daydreams. That's what most people use their minds for – their private entertainment: fantasies, "oughts" and "shoulds," hopes and wishes, daydreams, much like mental "selfies."

The only evidence you or anyone else has that you have any intentions is what you do about them in the real world. They do not exist in the real world unless and until you act upon them. There is nothing wrong with private fantasies if they serve you well. No one needs to know what you are thinking or feeling unless *you* feel the need to tell them. You can let your actions speak for you. Your intentions will be deduced from your actions. Your actions reveal (to others) what your intentions are. You can say to another person "I love you." But, unless the other person is terminally desperate, they will judge what your intentions are by how you comport yourself. The old adage is: *"Actions speak louder than words."* You can try words over and over again (a sure sign of insanity that managers are fond of). But the meaning of what you say or they interpret will always be in the actions that your words produce – never in the words themselves.

You can say to yourself – or even to others – that you intend one day to run the organization where you work.

But unless that happens, no one (including you) has any measure of the seriousness of your stated intention. Alexander the Great didn't spend much time talking about his intention to conquer the known world. He just set about doing it. That's often the only distinction there is between those who only talk about their intentions and those who are too busy carrying out their intentions to waste any time talking about them. Publishers tell us that the more people merely talk about their intention to write a book, the less likely it is to actually happen. Novelists prefer to write their novels in lieu of talking about what they "intend" to do.

Music psychologist Gary McPherson conducted a study of would-be musicians. What he found was that

> *"...the single biggest determinant of their* performance *was not how much they practiced, or any innate ability, but simply their degree of long-term commitment."*

In his book, *The Geography of Genius*, from which this is taken, the author Eric Weiner goes on to say:

> *"Those in it for the long haul played better than those who were not, even if the short-termers practiced more than the others. If the long-term committed practiced a lot, they improved* 400 per cent *more than the short-term committed."*

One study such as this does not make anything certain. But with respect to *intention,* is seems to confirm our understanding that people who have longer-term intentions achieve more in the real world than do people who have no more than short-term intentions. The hundreds of intentions that capture our attention every day are not likely to lead to any real achievement. It is our long-term intentions that pay off. Very few people have lifetime intentions. They are the ones we look at in awe. They must have better genes than we have, or more "talent." No. They simply have longer-term intentions than do the rest of us.

####

You also need to ponder carefully the fact that an intention is *not* an achievement. We may sometimes treat young children as if having an intention is some kind of achievement. It is not. What most distinguishes achievers from their peers is that they realize they have to be capable of carrying out any worthy long-term intention. They commit themselves to what is going to be required of them to carry out their intention. It may take years of study and practice to become a concert pianist, an Olympic contender, or a world-class ceramicist. It isn't the intention that gets you there, no matter how passionate you might be about it. It is your competence, your capability that gets you there. And that is where you begin to get where you intend to go. It may take years. And there may be many disappointments along the way. But a long-term commitment is just that: *a long-term commitment* – whatever it takes. There may be steps along the way. And they may become increasingly difficult. Please note carefully the commitment implicit in Epictetus's words (which you have seen before):

"First, say to yourself what you would be;
then do what you have to do."

Obviously, bedrock advice. You won't find such advice in any more succinct form. You could read a bevy of books about how to make a life. But the extra words do not make it any plainer. What makes Epictetus's advice about how to live the good life different is that he didn't spend his or your time "philosophizing." He tells you what to DO. Although sparse, his perspective on the good life rank with Buddhism's *Dhammapada* and Lao Tzu's *Tao Te Ching* as one of the greatest wisdom texts of human civilization. (If you want more, this is taken from his *The Art of Living*, as interpreted by Sharon LeBell.)

> *"When something happens, the only thing in your power is your attitude toward it; you can either accept it or resent it."*

You can't control the happening. All that is within your control is your attitude toward it. If you live by your intentions, you will invariably be thwarted. If you don't, things happen anyway. If obstacles occur, you have the prerogative of saying "Thank you" and moving on. If what happens makes your life better or your character, you have the prerogative of saying "Thank you" and moving on. More than this makes you a part of the problem.

Maybe you won't resent it. Maybe you will only be frustrated or angered. No matter. If your frustration or your anger get you to what you would be (highly unlikely), accept it. Otherwise the best attitude for you to adopt may be that of indifference. Say to the world: "I am doing what I have to do to be what I would be. I know, world, that you do not care one way or the other. But I do. And I will persist in order to be what I intend to be."

Intention can be strengthened, like anything else, by the adversity you encounter. Your intentions can outlive your adversity. The issue is whether or not you are committed. Commitment is commitment. What was it Yoda said? "There is no try. There is only do or do not." Just do what you have to do to be what you have chosen to be. See it through. That's the conception of intention that you need in order to live your life intentionally, rather than being victimized by what happens. Who understood this better than Thomas Edison?

Edison wanted to invent an incandescent light bulb in order to light up the world. His experiments failed, many times. But *he* did not. His attitude was "No, I didn't fail. I merely found 900 ways that don't work."
He persisted. The intention does not belong to the light bulb. It belongs to the human who invented it. And he either lived by his intention, or not. Persistence can win over "failure" in most situations.

####

So, again, it is not the worthiness or the rightness of your intention that matters (although many people who are misled by the pop culture may think so). Charlie Brown famously said (about his baseball "team"), "How can we fail when we are so sincere?"

Well, because sincerity doesn't DO anything. Even if you changed the word sincere to the word determined. Or, even if he had said, "How can we fail when we are so passionate to win?" These are internal states. But perhaps they were only words to make public their intention. Words – like determination and passion and sincerity – are intended to impress someone, perhaps the speaker. But words and states of mind do not DO anything. Doing something has to be accomplished in the real world. That is of course one of the problems of intention. It is a mental construct, therefore private and known only to the person who has the intention. People may think they have an intention to do this or that, but five minutes later they may have forgotten they ever had such an intention. There is no evidence of its existence apart from what the person says about it or does about it in the real world.

So it is easy to have "good" intentions (which, as the old saying goes, the road to hell is paved with). In our world, it's easy for a person to take credit for having good intentions, even though they were never carried out. That person (and often those around him or her) has an excuse: "I intended to do that." The good intention is accepted by oneself and others in lieu of a good *deed*. Is that what you would want to mean by *intention*? Or do you see it more like a motive?

If you think, as this book has suggested, that your worthy intentions acted upon are like pathways to your future destiny, then they become crucial to your life. But most people don't treat them that way. They become the matter for jokes, since we know that most people neither have worthy intentions nor have learned to carry them out. Is that because most people just don't care about their destinies, or the kind of lives that take them to worthy destinies? They are treated like a piece of clothing we bought, but never liked. For example, Evan Esar quipped:

> *"You are young only once – after that you have to think up some other excuse."*

Or:

> *"Children are always wasting time trying to convince their parents that it was someone else's fault."*

What is the life lesson the parents are trying to teach the child by engaging in this, or what is the lesson the children are trying to teach us by engaging in wasting time in this way? It takes two to carry on a conversation, just as it takes two to tango. So both the parent and the child are learning how to carry on this kind of conversation. If they do so three or four times, it will become a habit. Then they will be serving the habit and not their own best interests.

For anyone to use his or her intentions as pathways to their worthy future, their intentions have to be meaningful to them. First of all, they have to have some *worthy* purpose in mind for their lives, their destiny. Then they have to do conscious triage on their intentions: which ones are going to get them where they intend to go, and which ones, at the end of the day, won't have made any difference one way or the other. Many of our moment-to-moment intentions are like that. If they are something you must do – because they are necessary to your making a living, or because they are just part of your chores – do them, do them well, but do not dwell on them just as a convenient way of procrastinating your day away. Everyone has the same 24 hours you do. That's all Michelangelo had to work with. He just deflected the intentions that weren't going to get him where he wanted to go on that day. As we all know, he was an artist, a sculptor, an architect, and an engineer. If his intentions made him better at what he did, they were good intentions and he acted on them.

If not, he made himself immune to them. He didn't hang out with others much, unless he could learn something from them pertinent to his intentions.

Going to college is a bit like that. If you have decided what you want to be, you will find what you need there, and disregard the rest. Just because the menu is in front of you doesn't mean that everything is equally nutritious. Successful people make their intentions work for them because they have arrived at them intentionally – for their *worthy* purposes in life. If the marble Michelangelo had hand-picked himself broke, he didn't waste time talking about it. He knew that his time either contributed to his projects, or was wasted. So what contribution could talking about it make? The fault was his. So he moved on. You chose the college and you chose the course. Make it work for you or get on with your purposes in life. It is your fault you are there. There is no such thing as a boring course. There are only bored people. Do you have the time to waste by talking about it? You have a day at work which is full of distractions. If you can't make today work for you and your intentions in life, you have little hope for tomorrow.

Intentions can be potent – powerful. Or they can be irrelevant. Don't give the irrelevant much in the way of mindshare. Worthy intentions can give your life meaning and direction. Let them mark your way.

Some people think that what *they* pay attention to is "the world" they live in. This is the grand illusion. People see what they are capable of seeing. They never see the world as "it" is. They are stuck with seeing the world as they *are.* They have a unique, idiomatic perspective on the world which they mistake for "reality." Everything that "is" or happens in anyone's world has to be interpreted. You either accept others' interpretation (usually sourced in the pop culture) or you make up one of your own. How toxic or benign your world is depends upon how you interpret it. Nothing comes to you with its meaning inscribed on its back. You provide that. What people or things *mean* depends ultimately on what they mean to you. From the beginning of time, things and events and people have meant to people whatever they said those things meant. So you can – Don Quixote-like – make the world mean to you what you need it to mean to you. It was Quixote's intention to see the world *not as it appeared to be by others, but as it could be – ideally.* Is there any way to make it that way except by performing yourself in it *as if* it were that way? We might ask of ourselves: Which is the primary driver in your life – your "experiences" or your cause? At least that is what Cervantes had in mind – to alert us to the fact that, if we weren't entirely satisfied with our lives or our worlds, they are both open to change by *performing* one's life differently...in this case, *intentionally.*

As long as a person does not test his or her perspective on the world in the real world, they are free to construe their perspective any way they can for their private benefit. What one imagines doesn't affect the real world in any way. There is a lot of talk and many books and seminars these days about "life-making." But you can't do a good job of life-making unless you have a fairly accurate picture of what the real world is like. The first thing to learn about the real world (repeated from an earlier context) is this:

- *The real world doesn't care one way or the other about your intentions or what you choose to do about them. In fact, the real world doesn't care whether you live or die.*

- *If you want to make the real world more like it could be, there may be some interest in your intentions.*

- *If you want to make the world into a world more amenable to you personally, you may encounter daunting obstacles.*

- *If your intentions are not "worthy" – that is, not focused on leading the world to be a better place for deserving people other than you, your intentions are flawed at the outset.*

- *If you don't understand the real world well enough to know what it would take to fulfill your intentions, your intentions are likely to be stillborn. You can "wish upon a star." But the stars are not obligated to help you even if they could, which they cannot.*

- *If you persevere in trying to fulfill your worthy intentions, the real world may take notice. If you abandon your long-term intentions because they turned out not to be as easy as the pop culture made them out to be, who cares? The world will be here tomorrow whether you are or not.*

- *In other words, if you want or need someone or something to fulfill your intentions, they become hopeless.*

####

"Living As Intended" refers to *your* intentions, not the intentions the world has for you – if any. The potential obstacles notwithstanding, those who make a life using their worthy intentions as their trailblazers typically have remarkable lives. You can think of numerous inspiring examples from history: Queen Elizabeth, Queen Boudica, Alexander, Michelangelo, Lawrence of Arabia, even Leonard Bernstein. You have probably known a person who lived his or her life intentionally. That would not necessarily be the person who was "happiest." Happiness can be faked. It would have been the person who was never bored, who had little time for small talk, and who wasn't continuously looking for some "fun" to divert themselves (the pop culture), but who seemed most gratified by what they were accomplishing in their lives by letting their worthy intentions lead the way. They were fulfilled by their lives. They were self-empowered, just wanting more life in order to get on with their purposes. Maybe you remember this from George Bernard Shaw:

> *"This is the true joy in life, the being used for a purpose recognized by yourself as a mighty one...the being a force of nature instead of a feverish, selfish little clod of ailments and grievances complaining that the world will not devote itself to making you happy."*

The last phrase seems to be the refuge for many people. Did you ever meet anyone who said, "I really want to be just mediocre – like everyone else I know!" Even more people seem to believe that this is just a matter of individual choice. It isn't. It matters greatly who you hang out with in life. They will tell you who or what to be and do. It matters how widely you read. Because reading good books does two things: it enables you to think better next week than you did last week (it opens doors that were closed to you); and it enables you to grow and live beyond the small world of your immediate acquaintances. Get acquainted with Proust or with Shaw or with Nietzsche – not much discussed on the links or in the classroom. But that's the point. If you parley with them, you will be one of them. In short, your epistemic community matters – greatly. It is your immunity. Your "friends" don't bill themselves that way. But that's the point.

Does Shaw exaggerate? Of course. He wants to get your attention. Whose attention do you want to get – need to get? Yours? It has often been noticed by social critics that most people stumble through life in a kind of sleep-walking way: they find their comfort zone and spend the rest of their lives furnishing *that*. It was not their intention to live in their comfort zones. They had at one time intentions that would take them out of their comfort zones. What happened?

What happened was that they "settled" for what they had. They got to be content with who they were – because they had "friends" who didn't want them to change. Their "friends" blackmailed them: If you change, I won't be your friend anymore. They perhaps didn't say so. But that's what "friends" do. Did you ever have a "friend" who had no curiosity whatsoever about what it meant to be a friend (probably the second most common theme in all of the world's literature)? If you want to be someone's friend but are not curious about this peculiar thing – *friendship* – you will probably never be a good friend to anyone. You will be asking: What's in it for me? It's like "love." If you don't know how to really love someone, you probably don't deserve to be loved.

You may "intend" to be a good lover. But, as we have seen: if not worthy, if not acted upon, your intentions come to naught. "Naught" = zero. If your life is not one of exploring beyond your comfort zone, it is not a worthy life. And how do you do this? By your *worthy* intentions, acted upon. Is there any other way of understanding that? You grow by learning, not by knowing. You learn by having worthy intentions, and by the results of what you do about them. Collecting "knowledge" is roughly as valuable as collecting beer cans. What you need to learn you must learn by doing, as Aristotle suggested. So he is not one of your advisors? Why not? One might have thought you were serious about how you live. If you do not live by your intentions, then what's the point? Junk food – for the body or the mind – will make junk of your life.

Sad to say: But most people's lives contribute little or nothing of lasting value to other people or to the society. They're born, they do stuff that others do, they work for a living, and maybe they "retire." Their lives were not very meaningful to them, so their arrivals and departures in this world really mean very little of any consequence to the society. They may have procreated or enjoyed some years of sport sex or golfing or shopping. They were perhaps okay as consumers. But consumerism (if that was their guiding philosophy) makes little qualitative contribution to the destiny of the society beyond the status quo. We are like small candles that exist as long as we last. Then, as we saw earlier, we forget everything, and eventually so does everyone else. They did not ponder why they were here for a brief time. Coming from nothing meaningful, they return to that place of meaninglessness.

There is a difference between having "fun" and having fun doing something worthwhile – doing something that humanizes rather than dehumanizing us. Some people do not live by any ideal. They live by expediency, expecting to find a worthy cause for their lives in "the news," in their casual conversations, and in what they can buy – i.e., the size of their television sets or the cost of their shoes. They become pontificating experts on how to squander their lives which at one time held so much promise. In short, they live without worthy intentions and die with little to show for their lives beyond their bank accounts and their incidental grandchildren.

None of this denies their right to waste themselves like they waste the world. If they are "free," they are free to commit suicide in the most popular way. They begin as insatiably curious creatures. They end, for the most part, as sated creatures. Our pop culture does not believe in life. It believes in "knowledge." So people collect knowledge and pin it to their identities as they might pin butterflies in a collection. They could possibly pass a paper-and-pencil test on how to live – IF the test were based on the "knowledge" they were supposed to collect. But in real life there is no paper-and-pencil test. You *craft* your life. If it is handed to you by the pop culture as a recipe, you are doomed to live and die as most people do – *as if* it mattered not at all.

After your having pondered all of the above conscientiously...maybe it isn't supposed to matter. The birds and the bees live intentionally. But maybe that doesn't mean that we *people,* given our rational free will and all of our various philosophies, are obligated to live intentionally. Plants and trees live intentionally. But they can't do otherwise. We people think we can. We can live however we chose to live. We are not a part of nature. We are above nature. We can create our own nature by creating our multifarious cultures. For those of us who are, we can justify being omnivores. After all, we're "intelligent." We can eat the meat of (some) animals, and (some) plants, but not others. We're not supposed to eat one another, but some cultures think it is better than okay: If you eat the flesh of your enemies, you will gain their advantages in life. The bull cares not if he copulates with his daughter. Neither, apparently, does she. Some religions (all invented by people) would take a dim view of a father copulating with his daughter. We invent our languages, which provide us with proprietary worldviews. We wear different costumes for different purposes. No other critters we know of use cosmetics to change their appearance and, sometimes, failing that, we have cosmetic surgery to correct nature's mistakes. Our artifacts are *our* artifacts. We build bridges that collapse and cars to take us there. We design places to incarcerate our children on school days, and prisons to incarcerate people who are not law-abiding, even if those laws are propelling us to hell. People write stories about love, but seldom have readers or viewers gotten beyond lust. They quickly learn what sells. We have love-ins, but practice in our demonstrations hate-ins. We create worlds with our words. If our worlds don't fit with your worlds, we may have to annihilate you or, given our rampaging technology, both of us. We like our humanly-created gods, but only if they are of the same opinion we are about certain things. We kill in the name of peace. We befriend in the name of avarice. We want to control all nature but our own.

We create our worlds by how we explain them – past, present, or future. Every explanation comes from *some* perspective. Every explanation either encourages or discourages the evolution of further explanations. They hold for the people who hold them until a "better" explanation comes along. The American pop culture encourages "new" explanations over "old" explanations. In science and marketing alike, we believe in the obsolescence of "outdated" ideas and fashions in dress and comportment. Of course ideas are either fashionable or they are not. Diseases are either fashionable or they are not. What happens to diseases that (for one reason or another) go out of fashion? The same thing that happens to clothing or housing design that goes out of fashion? If we are not paying attention to something (the conundrum of quantum mechanics), does it exist?

What exists for us is what we are capable of or inclined to pay attention to in some way. Its existence depends upon our corroboration that it exists. (If you don't know what the protocols are in a given culture for conversations or dress, you are likely to make a *faux pas*.) You may have had a perspective but your perspective was not the current one. If you did fall asleep for twenty years, you would likely be disoriented in the world you once knew. What you say or do may no longer be politically correct. We say the world changes. Is that because the world changes or because our perspectives and thus our expectations of it have changed?
"Public opinion" is not what it was 25 years ago. That's *our* culture. If you happened to be Hopi, such changes were not likely to occur. That is because they had no comprehension of "public opinion" – which therefore did not exist. If you had never ever heard of "love" in your culture, could you fall into it?

In her theater piece (1985, performed by Lily Tomlin), *The Search for Signs of Intelligent Life in the Universe,* Jane Wagner wrote:

> *"What is reality anyway?! It's nothing but a collective hunch."*

It may be a collective hunch by scientists or your neighborhood klatch. What makes it seem authoritative is the "collective" part of it. In one cult or culture, sex may be taboo. In another, it may be rampant. In one cult or culture, pork may be taboo. In another, it may be a basic food. Many cultures do not have a golf course. In another, golf may be the center of life for rich people. In some cultures, there may be rich people and poor people. In another, there may only be poor people. In some cultures, people may be "illiterate." But you got here even if your parents were not very smart. They were smart enough to procreate and to survive. (Do we do either one that much better?) Otherwise, you would not be here. In some cultures, there is no such thing as "depression." In ours, you could get rich treating that condition. So, indeed it could hardly be doubted that people create their cultures and then those cultures create them (a variation on Churchill and buildings). It is the pop culture that influences us, no longer any "reality." In any case, beliefs have always been more influential than any "facts."

And if we don't know where we are going, we may end up someplace else. This was, I think, Wagner's point. The perspective is that of a street person, unseen by most. But does anyone have a better perspective on life than a person who doesn't really have one according to us?

She's the ultimate alien, the one closer to "reality" than any of the rest of us.

Or, there is Mal Hancock's cartoon balloon in the *San Francisco Sunday Examiner & Chronicle* (of 25 February 1990):

"Reality is the ultimate illusion"

What does that mean to a person who believes in "reality"? It's like the warning on a pack of cigarettes. If you are a smoker, you don't pay any attention to it. If you are a non-smoker, you may read it and even feel "healthier." Re Hancock above: if you are a believer in "reality" and in "facts," you will gloss over it as being nonsense. If you are a believer in poetry or metaphor, you will nod in agreement. Is the disagreement about reality? Or is the disagreement about belief? Scientist or atheist, intellectual or ignoramus, we believe what we believe, and that is our *reality*.

So the first question is: Is your belief in your reality – or anything else – good for you or not good for you...and your personal destiny? Good for the larger society or not good for the larger society and *its* destiny?

The second question is: Do you intend to make a contribution of a good life to the larger society, or do you intend to contribute negatively (in one or more various ways) to the larger society?

The third question is: If you have worthy (efficacious) intentions, are you capable and committed to acting on them?

That would explicate what is meant here by Living As Intended. If you live as intended, you will have no regrets. If you don't, you will little by little start living regretfully. The most glorious life is probably living your dreams (assuming they are worthy). The next best would seem to be living by some ideals – which today might be called "principles." If you shy away from the ideal, you shy away from a life of living as intended. In the end, the life you have lived *is* your legacy. You may have 100 cars and a billion dollars at the end of life but you will still be measured by your positive influence on others, and thus your contribution to the larger society. The ultimate illusion is believing it might be anything else.

It will be who you were as a *person*, and how your *ideals* lifted others to a more ideal – a better – life. This is the measure, whether you lived at the top or the bottom. If that is not what you intended, your own life will have been in vain.

14 Epilogue

Life is a project. You are, by choice or by default, the project *manager* of your life. There is no one else who can do it. Perhaps there is no one else who would want the job. Many people abdicate the role midway, or earlier.

It comes down to how capable you can make yourself as the manager of that project. It comes down to what your intentions are with respect to your life – the only one you will have, and the only time you will ever have it.

In a "free" country, what you intend to do with it is up to you. But not completely...in our contemporary world. It's also up to what your parents and the other adults who raised you intended for you. It's also up to the intentions of your friends, your teachers, your mentors and your models. It's also up to the pop culture you imbibe, whether those influences come to you directly or indirectly. Your life has many guidance systems competing for control of your life. The most critical one is of course who you are and how you think about things. Depending on those influences by others, you will harbor beliefs and opinions – private "theories" about how things work and why. All these will put your life and *keep* your life on a trajectory – a life's story, your story. Unless *you* change it by bartering what you are for what you intend to be. The story you weave will either be good for you, or not good for you. How you live your life will either be good for other people and the larger society, or not good for them. They will repay the efficacy of your life in kind.

Bad people think the world is bad. Good people think the world is good. They are both wrong. The world is what it is. Circumstances are what they are. Good is what it is because bad is what it is, and vice versa. The world is how a person sees it. The world that you participate in is a virtual world. It exists in the minds of the people who agree with you or disagree with you. Scientists see the world they expect to see, with or without the intervention of the instruments *they* have invented to look at it – whether the cosmos or your gizzard. The only real difference between an ancient human and a contemporary human are the techniques employed (or not) to justify their (or our) perspective. You can believe anything you want to. The "world" won't care. There may be some *people* who want to eliminate you from this world to prove they are right and you are wrong. But the "world" we know could care less about what we want to believe or what we intend to do about it. And no one person can change it in any significant way – except perhaps for Drucker's view that there have been only three leaders in modern times: Hitler, Mao, and Stalin. The question remains: Isn't there some "nicer" and more rational way of making an impact on the world?

This book says yes there is. As conceptualized herein.

Goethe offered a pertinent and profound perspective on life-making (in or out of organizations) when he wrote:

> *"You should love people not for what they are, but for what they could be."*

Two things to ponder here:

- One is that if you are one of what are called "people," this applies equally and first of all to you. You must approve of yourself not for what you are, but for what you could (or *should)* be. This involves your intentions – a future aim. Your *life* is not successful just because you have achieved some success at something in your life. Your life is successful if you are still striving for the ideal *you* – at any age. Life-making is about the ongoing *pursuit* of the ideal, not about having adapted like a victim to your present circumstances.

- The other is that you cannot change the world. You change your immediate world only by changing the way you perform in it. If you insist upon being what you are and asking someone else to change the world to suit you, you are a false lover of yourself. What *should* you be? This is the question Epictetus raised and then offered to map a way. This is the question we have tried to raise here, and to answer by mapping a way, whatever your *worthy* intentions may be. You cannot become what you intend to be without bartering what you are for what you ought to be. You cannot change the world you know for a better world unless you become a better person.

No one knows what the logic is that dictates that process. But you will find no alternative. You exist only in the world you know. To change that you must become the person you intend to be.

You grow and evolve by your intentions, acted upon. If they are not yours, they will be someone else's. That is not living by intention, but by default.

CPSIA information can be obtained
at www.ICGtesting.com
Printed in the USA
LVHW101506200122
708999LV00023B/1000/J